TWOPENCE TO CROSS THE M[illegible]

Helen Forrester was born i[illegible] the eldest of seven c[illegible] until she marrie[illegible] city that features p[illegible] the past forty years [illegible]ta, Canada.

Helen Forrester is t[illegible]hor of four bestselling volumes of autobiography and a number of equally successful novels, including most recently *Madame Barbara.* In 1988 she was awarded an honorary D.Litt. by the University of Liverpool in recognition of her achievements as an author. The University of Alberta conferred on her the same honour in 1993.

By Helen Forrester

Fiction

THURSDAY'S CHILD
THE LATCHKEY KID
LIVERPOOL DAISY
THREE WOMEN OF LIVERPOOL
THE MONEYLENDERS OF SHAHPUR
YES, MAMA
THE LEMON TREE
THE LIVERPOOL BASQUE
MOURNING DOVES
MADAME BARBARA

Non-Fiction

TWOPENCE TO CROSS THE MERSEY
LIVERPOOL MISS
BY THE WATERS OF LIVERPOOL
LIME STREET AT TWO

HELEN FORRESTER

TWOPENCE TO CROSS THE MERSEY

TED SMART

HarperCollins*Publishers*
77–85 Fulham Palace Road,
Hammersmith, London W6 8JB

www.harpercollins.co.uk

This edition produced for The Book People Ltd,
Hall Wood Avenue, Haydock, St Helens WA11 9UL

This paperback edition 1993

First published in Great Britain by
Jonathan Cape Ltd 1974
Reissued by The Bodley Head 1979

ISBN 0 00 775003 X

Set in New Baskerville

Printed and bound in Great Britain by
Clays Ltd, St Ives plc

To the Liverpool City Police

CHAPTER ONE

Liverpool is a city through which visitors pass on their way to other places. It is to them a dull world of shipping and commerce which sprawls untidily along the north bank of the River Mersey. Many of them will not know that it has a sister port, Birkenhead, on the opposite bank, which is linked to it by ferry-boats, a railway tunnel and a road tunnel. Beyond Birkenhead lie the small seaside towns of the Wirral peninsula and behind them is pleasant countryside. My widowed grandmother lived in the Wirral, and here, while visiting her, I spent the happiest days of my childhood, on sandy beaches or in wind-swept gardens. I remember with love the rain-soaked hills looking out on to stormy seas and the turbulent estuary of the Mersey.

It used to cost twopence to cross the river on

the ferry-boat from Liverpool to Birkenhead. Twopence is not a very large sum, but if one has no money, the river is a real barrier, and, during the Depression years, was an impassable one to many of the poverty-stricken people of Liverpool.

Not so many years ago, I took my little Canadian-born son to see Liverpool and the places of my childhood.

'Did you live here when you were small, Ma?' he asked incredulously, his strong North American accent sounding strange amid the thick, nasal speech around him.

'Yes, I was in Liverpool for part of my life.'

'My, it's dirty! Do you mind it being dirty?'

I smiled, seeing it all through his stranger's eyes, eyes accustomed to new buildings, miles of neon signs, miles of prairie golden with wheat or diamond-white with snow.

I laughed down at him a little ruefully.

'Yes, at first I did mind. Not now, though. I soon learned that people and cities which do the hard, unpleasant work of the world can't help getting dirty. Liverpool's a wonderful place when you get to know it.'

He looked at me derisively and said, with all the cold logic of a five-year-old, 'They should use more soap and – wash the streets.'

My smile faded, as cold shadows of winters past crept over me. That was how I had felt, when first I had really looked at the city and not passed through it as a traveller. God, how I had minded the dirt! How terrified I had been! How menacingly grotesque the people had looked; children of the industrial revolution, nurtured for generations on poor food in smoke-laden air, grim and twisted, foul-mouthed and coarse, shaped in this strange gloomy world to serve the trade to the Americas. And I, a middle-class girl of the gentler south-west of England who had been shielded from the rougher side of life by a private school system and obedient servants, had nearly gone mad with panic when, with little warning, I had been thrown amongst them. Gone was the protection of money and privilege; I had to make what I could of this grimy city and its bitterly humorous inhabitants and share with them their suffering during the Depression years.

I clutched my son's confiding little hand in mine, as, for a second, I felt again the fear which had enveloped me that January day in 1931, when, at the age of twelve and a half, I arrived in Liverpool, not to pass through it as I had done before, but to live in it.

It seemed to me that it was not my son's hand

which I held so tightly but the hand of my youngest sister, Avril, and that I could hear her snivelling, as we looked out from the entrance of Lime Street Station and saw, through icy, driving rain, a city which seemed to be slowly dying, unloved and unsung, in the Depression of the nineteen-thirties.

CHAPTER TWO

'Shut up, Avril,' I said sternly, between chattering teeth. 'Everything is going to be all right.'

'I'm cold and I'm hungry.' The wail threatened to become one of three-year-old Avril's howling tantrums, as she started to kick off her patent-leather shoes and tear at her blue satin bonnet-strings.

I loosened the wet elastic of my black school hat from under my chin. The hat, as usual, had been crammed down on top of a large ribbon bow, which held my front hair ruthlessly scraped back from a too high forehead. My spectacles were sprayed with rain and I could not see very well as I peered short-sightedly down Lime Street.

I lifted Avril up and hugged her to my damp school uniform.

'Behave yourself,' I ordered sharply. 'We are all hungry. You must be brave until Daddy comes back to collect us.'

Fortunately, I did not know that my father, at that moment walking the streets of Liverpool in search of shelter for his sick wife and seven children, had no real idea of what to do to mitigate the catastrophe which had struck him. I presumed that adults always knew what they were doing and the likely outcome of their actions. I did not know that my mother, lying on a stretcher in the ladies' waiting-room, her six-week-old son beside her, was sweating with pain after a major abdominal operation and was bordering on a nervous breakdown. I could not understand why we could not go to stay with my grandmother, who lived only a few miles away in the Wirral peninsula. No one had told me she had quarrelled violently with her son and his wife, whom she condemned jointly as worthless spendthrifts, and would have no more to do with us.

Busy with childish affairs of school and girlfriends, I had noticed only that during the last few weeks my parents' friends were not dropping in for a drink as frequently as usual; in fact the house had been almost free of visitors for a couple of months.

Alan, who was a year younger than I, had

pointed out to me a few months earlier that Mother's wonderful collection of Georgian silver had vanished from the antique sideboard on which it was normally displayed, and I had asked my mother where it had gone.

'Girls should not poke their noses into the business of grown-ups,' I had been told tartly, and I had retreated to Alan for consolation.

'Perhaps it has been sold,' he had whispered uneasily, as he ran his fingers through his corn-coloured hair.

'Why?' I asked, my eyes goggled in surprise.

He stared at me reflectively, his wide, blue eyes troubled. 'I don't know. There is something wrong. Mary Ann packed her suitcase and left on Saturday.'

Mary Ann was our housemaid, a jolly, outspoken girl.

'I thought she had gone home to visit her mother for a few days – that's what she told me.'

'I don't think so. She seems to have taken everything with her. She even asked Cook for her curling-tongs back – Cook was always borrowing them.'

Our uneasiness grew while Mother was in hospital, until an idle word from a school-friend gave us a clue.

Father had done a mysterious thing called 'going bankrupt', a not uncommon occurrence in the world of 1930, but strange to me. I had heard vaguely that going bankrupt was an American disease which had struck Wall Street in New York, and that Americans committed suicide when this happened to them; mentally, I saw dozens of them hurling themselves off the tops of skyscrapers, and I wondered where Father would find a skyscraper.

Father was a public school man who had been sent to boarding school by his widowed mother when he was only six years old; he had left it at nineteen to join the army in 1914. My mother, an orphan, had been brought up by nuns. Neither had had any training in the management of a family or a domestic budget, and they had enjoyed a high standard of living by being permanently in debt. Further, they had had seven children. Bankruptcy was inevitable, once the Depression set in and dividends dried up.

The remainder of our servants left in a body, while Mother was still in hospital, and I was left to manage the home as best I could, until we moved to Liverpool. One of our unpaid domestics took the opportunity, while my parents were absent, to take away my mother's entire wardrobe, leaving her only the outfit she had been wearing when she was whisked into hospital.

Father had no knowledge of the legal rights of a bankrupt to clothing and bedding, so he sent the key of our house to his main creditor, a moneylender, with instructions to sell the house and its contents, and to reimburse himself from the proceeds. From a misguided sense of honour, he left everything we possessed, except the clothing in which he and his family were dressed, taking only a pair of blankets in which to wrap my mother and the new baby, Edward. Then, with his last ten pounds in cash, he bought tickets on the train to Liverpool, which was his birthplace.

He remembered Liverpool as a bustling, wealthy city and hoped to find employment there, perhaps as an accountant, in a shipping company. Having lived for years in prosperous, southern market-towns, he could not visualize what the Depression was doing to the north of England. He could not imagine that a man who desired work would not be able to find it.

Liverpool looked a dreadfully dismal place to my untutored eyes. Water swirled along the gutters, carrying a horrid collection of garbage. Across the road, the fine Corinthian pillars of St George's Hall looked like a row of rotting teeth, and to my right, down William Brown Street, marched a series of equally large, black buildings. When I peeked farther out of the station I could see the entrance of a big theatre, the Empire, and farther along at the corner was a public house, the Legs o' Man, near which a number of seamen stood laughing and joking, oblivious of the rain. Much later on, a sailor told me that sooner or later everybody in the world passed the Legs o' Man and if you waited long enough you could meet there anybody you cared to look for; certainly, it was a great meeting-place.

Along the pavement men in shabby cloth caps shuffled from litter-bin to litter-bin to sift through the garbage for food and cigarette-ends. In the gutter stood four unemployed Welsh miners, caps held hopefully out while they sang over and over again in sad tenor voices 'Land of our Fathers' and 'All through the Night'.

'Are you lost?'

I jumped and Avril stopped wailing. A policeman, water running down his cape and helmet, was bending over us, his red face concerned.

'No, thank you,' I said primly, and, since he continued to look down at us doubtfully, I added, 'Mummy is in the waiting-room.'

He smiled in a friendly fashion.

'Better go back to her, luv,' he said, 'Lime Street is no place for a nice young lady – and ye'll get wet.'

Reluctantly, I retraced my steps to the waiting-room.

Father had been away four hours or more. Baby Edward had not been fed and was crying lustily. Brian and Tony, aged six and five respectively, were playing tag round and round the high, varnished benches. Despite his determined effort at playing, I could see that Brian was afraid. Taut and dark as an Indian, so highly strung that he suffered constantly from nightmares, his little hands were clenched tight and his heart-shaped face was grim. Tony was playing the game with his usual cool care, watching his elder brother closely so as to anticipate every move he made. His mind seemed to work with such intelligence that it was as if he had been born with a brain already mature and furnished with knowledge. Sometimes when I stroked his silky, flaxen head I was almost unnerved by the idea of the latent power beneath my hand.

Fiona, aged nine, was still sitting silently by my mother, nursing her favourite doll, her huge, pale-blue eyes wide with dumb fear. We all loved Fiona with unquestioning devotion. She never had tantrums as Avril and I did; she never seemed to get dirty or forget her table manners. I always had a book in my hand, hated to miss school and loved an argument; Fiona adored her large doll family, accepted school but learned little. She was our placid refuge when we had been spanked, which was not infrequently, but now *she* needed asylum.

Mother lay on the stretcher, her eyes closed, her face ethereally white. An empty teacup on the bench beside her spoke of the kindness of the lavatory attendant, who stood leaning against her cupboard door, smoking a cigarette and regarding us curiously. There was no one else in the waiting-room.

None of us had eaten since breakfast, a meal of toast hastily consumed, and now it was after four o'clock. I knew that my mother had no money in her handbag, so it was no good offering to go and buy something to eat from the station restaurant.

I went up to my mother. A tear lay on her cheek.

'Are you all right, Mummy?'

'Yes, dear. I got up and walked for a few moments a little while ago.'

'You'll soon be better, Mummy?'

'Yes – yes, I have to be.'

I picked Edward up from beside her and, holding him against my shoulder, tried to stop his healthy bellows for food by walking up and down with him and patting his tiny back.

Alan had been kneeling on a bench by the window, watching the horses and drays in the station yard. Now he came and walked with me. We did not talk; both our hearts were too heavy.

I knew that Mother had been ill after Edward was born and had been in hospital until Christmas Eve, a scant eight days ago. I realized, with a sense of shock, that Christmas and New Year had passed uncelebrated, lost in a foggy nightmare of quarrels, recrimination and general disorder in the house. Mother had discharged herself from hospital, before the doctors thought she should, so that we could come to Liverpool.

As I clucked sympathetically at Edward, it seemed madness to me to embark on such a journey. I could not understand why the moneylender could not wait a few days more before taking legal action, so that Mother could get a little stronger before she moved. I had no conception of the panic gripping my parents, a panic which had made them lose completely any sense of proportion. They had been brought up in a little world of moneyed people, insulated by their private means from any real difficulties or hardships. When there was no money, they had no idea what to do, beyond trying to obtain a 'suitable' position. A moneylender was, to them, a ruthless Scrooge, and I do not think that it occurred to them that if he had been apprised of Mother's illness he might have had a little compassion. And so they compounded their troubles to an unnecessary degree.

My relief was overwhelming when my father, soaking wet, came into the waiting-room, with a muttered apology to the attendant. He went straight to my mother. She opened her eyes and surveyed him sullenly.

'I have obtained two rooms. Not very good. Just for a week.' He sounded breathless and on edge. 'Had to pay in advance. Walked back. I'm going to get a cab.'

My mother closed her eyes, and my heart sank. They were trying not to talk to one another again.

Father vanished again into the vast cavern of the station, and Mother told me to help the boys get their overcoats on.

A few minutes later, Mother was carried on the stretcher with the aid of a porter to a taxi-cab, the children trailing behind and the baby and Avril still crying. The procession caused some interest in the station, and I remember my face burning with embarrassment under the shadow of my velour school hat. Well-bred people, I had

had it drummed into me, did not draw attention to themselves.

Mother crawled into the cab, and the porter folded up the stretcher, which belonged to the railway company. Somehow we all squeezed into the taxi, a hungry, forlorn group too tired to talk.

CHAPTER THREE

A stout, untidy blonde opened the door to us. A suffocating odour of unwashed bodies, old cooking and cats rolled over us. The woman beamed at us, however, and welcomed Father like an old friend. She helped him assist Mother into a room so shabby and so dirty that I could honestly say that I had never seen anything like it before. Next to it was a bedroom with two double beds crammed into it. There were no sheets or pillow-cases, just greasy pillows and grey blankets.

Mother sank on to a broken settee, while our landlady looked us over.

'You can keep coal out back and use t' kitchen and bathroom. There's eight other tenants upstairs and me and me sons on the top floor, so keep as quiet as yer can.' Her battered face showed pity. 'Ah'll give yer enough coal to start a fire. Coalman'll be along the street this afternoon and you can get some then.'

The room was very cold and Mother looked round it disdainfully, but she said. 'Thank you' in response to this offer of fuel.

'Come on, luv,' the landlady addressed me. 'There's a booket in that cupboard. We'll fill it and you can bring it back.'

After a trip through linoleumed passages and a littered, stinking kitchen to a coal-house by the back door, I staggered back with a bucket of coal, some wood chips and a newspaper. After much anxious effort, Father got a fire going. It was the first time he had ever made a fire.

Tony and Brian, usually the best of friends, had been bickering irritably for some time, and they now turned on Alan, who was himself fretful with hunger. Furiously, he cuffed the younger boys and made them cry.

Father snapped at him to stop.

Alan, usually so cheerful, stopped, and said heavily, 'When shall we be able to have something to eat?'

'How much money have you?' asked Mother. She had sat silently staring into space, while we had divested ourselves of our coats and Father had lit the fire.

Father went through his pockets, and laid the results of his search on the settee, so that we could see the small pile of coins in the light of the bare electric bulb hanging from the ceiling.

'Two and ninepence,' he announced helplessly.

Thirty-three precious pennies would buy quite a lot in those days, though they would not last long in a family the size of ours.

In a dull monotone, Mother upbraided him bitterly about the mess he had got us all into, and Father snarled back that she had never been any help to him. Finally, Edward's wailing drew his attention to more immediate concerns, and he said, 'There is a little corner shop down the road. We could at least get some milk for Edward.'

'And for me,' said Avril, thrusting her small chin aggressively forward.

'Be quiet, Avril,' I hissed, afraid that my parents would start to quarrel again.

'Won't,' replied Avril defiantly, but she did keep quiet thereafter.

Finally, it was decided that since Father was already wet through he might as well get a bit more wet by going out to the shop and buying all the food he could for the money he had.

When he had departed, the children crouched around the miserable fire, and Mother managed to change Edward's nappy. We had only three nappies with us, and the baby had not been changed since we had set out that morning. He was, therefore, in a disgusting condition. Mother gave me the nappy she had removed, told me to find the bathroom, wash the dirty garment and bring it back to dry by the fire. I wandered off, sick and dejected, and did the best I could with cold water and no soap in a Victorian bathroom which stank of half a century of neglect.

Afterwards, Alan and I went to the kitchen, where a few dust-covered dishes were strewn along open shelves. We collected them and washed them under the only tap and, with frozen fingers, carried them back to our room. With nervous and uncertain gestures, we laid them on the table, which was covered with torn, stained oilcloth. We also had hopefully brought with us a saucepan and a frying-pan, since there was no stove in the kitchen on which to cook.

Our spirits rose when Father returned with milk, two loaves of bread, margarine, tea, sugar and a small packet of sausages. He had also brought a twopenny packet of Woodbines. With cigarettes in their mouths, our parents became a little more civil to each other.

Under Mother's instructions, I made a feed for Edward and then fed him: he was ravenous and took the whole small bottle full. Father cooked sausages on the smoking fire, found a knife in the kitchen and cut the bread and spread it with margarine. We sat around on whatever we could find and ate a sausage apiece in our fingers. He managed to boil a pan of water and make tea in it. Mother drank much and ate little, refusing a sausage which was happily snatched up by Avril. Father finally ate, and only afterwards I realized that he had not had a sausage, and I felt a crushing sense of guilt about it.

Our landlady called down the stairs to say that she could hear the coalman coming, and my father looked aghast. The coal donated by our landlady was already nearly consumed and we had exactly a penny left. We could do nothing, and sat hopelessly silent, as the shout of 'Coal, coal, one and nine a hundredweight' faded down the street.

That was the first of many years of nights I spent tossing restlessly, napping, waking, unable to settle because of cold or gnawing hunger. Four of us, still dressed in our underwear, were packed somehow into one bed, and Father, Alan and Brian were to manage in the other bed. Mother stayed on the settee with the baby. For a long time I lay and listened to my parents quarrelling with each other, while the baby whimpered and Fiona, her head against my shoulder, chattered inconsequently in her own uneasy sleep, her doll clasped tightly to her. I fell into a doze, from which I was awakened by Mother calling me in the early morning. I was glad to leave the bed, which smelled of urine, put on my gym-slip and blouse and go to her.

It had been decided, she said, that Father should enrol Alan, Fiona, Brian and Tony at an elementary school he had noticed on his way to the corner shop the previous night. I was to stay at home and help with the baby. My loud protest that I would get behind with my schooling was sharply hushed. I was to see the children washed and tidied for school and was to divide the remaining bread and margarine between them for breakfast. All this I did, whilst shivering with cold. Brian and Tony were also shivering and were scared of going to school; Fiona and Alan were frankly relieved at the thought of something normal creeping back into their lives.

A breakfastless Father was gone with them for an hour and came back to report the children safely ensconced. He had put into his pocket, when leaving home, an old-fashioned cut-throat razor, and he now did his best to shave with it, in cold water, without soap. The result was not very good, and his clothing, still wet from yesterday's soaking, looked crumpled and old. He then departed for the employment exchange, a three-mile walk.

Mother, Avril and I sat almost silent in the icy room. Occasionally, we would feed the baby a little of the remaining milk. We warmed it slightly by putting the bottle next to Mother's skin down the front of her dress, and we wrapped the baby in Mother's coat, which had not got much wetted the previous day. I then tucked our two precious blankets round both mother and child. I longed to get out of the fetid room, even if it was only to stand at the front door, but I was too afraid of my mother in her present state to ask permission to do so.

The other children came home for lunch, but there was no lunch, and they departed again for school, cold, hungry and in tears, even brave Alan's lips quivering. Mother, Avril and I, like Father, had neither eaten nor drunk.

The afternoon dragged on and the children returned, except for Fiona.

'Fiona's ill,' explained Alan anxiously. 'A teacher is going to bring her home in a little while, when she feels better.'

I suppose my mother was past caring, for she

said nothing, but, to the griping hunger pains in my stomach, was added a tightening pain of apprehension for Fiona, the frailest of us all. I tried, however, to be cheerful while I helped the boys off with their coats and then put them on again immediately, because they said they were so cold.

The front door bell clanged sonorously through the house. I expected to hear the clatter of our landlady coming down the stairs to open it, but there was no sound from the upper regions of the house, so very diffidently I rose and answered it.

At the door, stood an enormously tall man in long, black skirts. In his arms he carried Fiona.

CHAPTER FOUR

I quailed before the apparition on the doorstep – it reminded me of an outsize bat and my over-stimulated imagination suggested that it might be a vampire; in the chaotic mess that our world had become, anything was possible. The voice that issued from the apparition's bearded face was, however, gentle and melodious, and asked to see my mother.

Nervously, I invited him (it was obviously male, despite the long, black dress) into the hall, and he slid a whey-faced Fiona to the floor, while I went to see Mother. She told me to bring the gentleman into our room, and, for the first time since our arrival, a slight animation was apparent in her face.

He entered, leading Fiona by the hand, and immediately my mother assumed the gracious manner which had, in the past, contributed to her reputation as an accomplished hostess.

'Father!' Her voice was bell-like. 'This is a pleasure! Come in. Do sit down.' She ignored poor Fiona, who came and stood by me, and stared dumbly at our new-found friend.

'Father'? It was beyond me. I had never seen an Anglican priest in high church robes, nor yet a Roman Catholic one, in the small towns in which we had previously lived. I stood, with fingers pressed against my mouth, and wondered what further troubles this visit portended.

He was explaining to Mother that the school was an Anglican Church school. After Fiona had come out of her faint, the headmistress had wormed out of her something of what was happening to us, and had then telephoned him. The advent of four well-dressed, well-behaved children entering a slum school had already caused some stir among the teachers and considerable jeering and cat-calling among the other pupils, so the headmistress had asked him to call upon us. Here he was, he announced gravely, and could he be of help?

As I examined the beautiful, serene face of the young priest, Mother poured out a condensed version of the story of Father's losses. He was a

Liverpool man originally, she said, and had come back to his native city in the hope of earning his living there. To me, the well-edited tale still presented a picture of foolishness, extravagance and carelessness.

Now, at last, I knew why we were in Liverpool and what the word 'bankruptcy' really meant to our family. I knew, with terrible clarity, that I would never see my bosom friend, Joan, again, never play with my doll's house, never be the captain of the hockey team or be in the Easter pageant. My little world was swept away.

I looked at Alan, who was standing equally silently by the window. His eyes met mine and we shared the same sense of desolation. Then his golden eyelashes covered his eyes and shone with tears, half-hidden.

'Have you no relations who would help you?' asked the priest.

'I have no relations,' said Mother coldly, 'and my husband's refused to know us at present.'

The priest combed his beard with his fingers, and smiled when Avril tried to reach up to touch it. He took her hand gently and held it, and within thirty seconds she had established herself triumphantly on his knee, from which safe throne she surveyed the rest of the family gleefully.

'There is a great deal of unemployment in Liverpool,' he said. 'I fear your husband may find difficulty in finding work.'

Mother just stared disconsolately at him.

At that moment Father entered, dragging his feet slowly and looking almost as hopeless as Mother. The children ignored him, the exhausted baby slept.

Desperate to fill the silence, I cried gladly, 'Daddy!'

He managed to smile faintly.

Mother introduced him formally to the priest, and he sat down and waited politely to hear why the priest was there. This was explained to him, while he shivered with cold and rubbed his blue hands together to restore the circulation.

Finally, the priest said to him, 'First things first. You must have a fire or your youngest child will die. Probably I can persuade old Wright to bring up a hundredweight of coal. I have some small funds and I will bring some food. After you have eaten perhaps I can advise you a little.'

He put his hand out over the children's heads in a gesture of blessing, said goodbye, strode out of the room and let himself out of the house.

The boys immediately broke into jubilant conversation with each other at the idea of food, and gradually Father began to relax a little for the same reason, though his face looked pinched and white. He had spent hour upon hour in the employment exchange, being chivvied from one huge queue to another, until he had finally got himself registered for work as a clerk. He was not eligible for unemployment insurance as he had never contributed to that fund, and the employment exchange clerk just laughed when he asked when he might hope to be sent to apply for a job. There were, he said, a hundred men for every job, and my father's age was a grave difficulty – at thirty-eight he was too old to hope seriously for employment.

He had hardly finished telling us of his adventures, when the doorbell rang again. I answered it quickly this time.

A surly voice from beneath a large hump inquired where it should put t' coal, and not to keep 'im waiting cos 'e 'adn't all night to run after folks as 'adn't enough sense to get it in the daytime.

The landlady had shown me where our coal could be stored, and the coalman clomped through the house behind me, scattering slack liberally around him, and heaved the coal expertly over his head, out of the sack and into a broken-down box in an out-house. Then, still muttering about improvident folks, he stomped back through the passage and departed into the darkness.

I flew in to Mother, and it seemed no time at all before we had a huge fire glowing, with Father's coat and jacket and Edward's nappy steaming in front of it. The already heavy atmosphere of the room was intensified by the cloying stench of these garments drying, but we did not care. We learned then that, when one has to choose between warmth and being half-fed, except in the last extremities of starvation, warmth is the better choice.

An hour later the priest presented himself again, carrying two large boxes and accompanied by a boy carrying two more. The boy dropped his burdens on the step and trotted away. The priest came in, at my shy invitation. He smiled at the sight of the comforted children kneeling by the fire between the drying clothes, and, with Father's aid, he unpacked the boxes.

The table was soon loaded with six loaves of bread, oatmeal, potatoes, sugar, margarine, a tin of baby milk, two bottles of milk, salt, bacon, some tea, a bar of common soap, a pile of torn-up old sheeting (for cleaning, and for the baby, he explained apologetically) and, wonder of wonders, a towel, a big one.

The priest sat down, and called the boys to him,

while Father and I made baby formula and porridge, and Alan collected all the dishes he could find. It felt oddly like a Christmas celebration, and even Mother seemed to come a little out of her apathy as she sipped the tea and ate the porridge Father eventually brought to her. I fed the baby while the children stuffed themselves with porridge, bread and margarine and chattered excitedly, Avril's shrill falsetto and Brian's contralto occasionally emerging from the general hubbub. At the priest's insistence, Father and I finally ate, and Father became more his old, lively self.

We boiled another panful of water, and I took Fiona, Brian, Tony and Avril to the bathroom, and washed their hands, faces and knees. They had not had their underclothes off for thirty-six hours and did not smell very sweet, even after my washing efforts, but a quart of water does not go very far in washing four people, and I reasoned that the beds stank so much that they were bound to smell by morning no matter what I did.

Afterwards I took them into the bedroom, tucked their overcoats over them, covered these with a greasy blanket, heard their prayers, and returned to Alan and my parents.

CHAPTER FIVE

Unemployment was so rampant in Liverpool that the young priest felt it necessary to warn Father that getting work would be a very slow process – he was too kind to say that it would be virtually impossible. He suggested that Father should apply for parish relief.

'What is that?' asked Father.

'Well, it is really the old poor-law relief for the destitute, but it is now administered by the city through the public assistance committee. More help is given by way of allowances rather than by committal to the workhouse.'

Father went white at the mention of the workhouse. I stared in shocked horror at the priest. I had read all of Charles Dickens's books – I knew about workhouses.

'I see,' said Father, his voice not much more than a whisper. 'I suppose I have no alternative.'

The priest asked about our accommodation, and sat, drumming his finger-tips upon his skirt-clad knee, when he was told that our landlady wanted her rooms back for another tenant, at the end of the week.

At last he spoke.

'There are a lot of older houses in the south end of the city. You might find a couple of rooms in one of those. Some of them are still quite respectable. There is also a High Church school in that area, which is a little better than an ordinary board school. However, you might have to pay twopence a week for each child at the school – and that might pose a problem.'

Father said optimistically that he could not imagine such a small amount being a problem, once we got settled.

The priest smiled at him pityingly, opened his mouth to speak and then decided otherwise. We would soon learn.

'Would you like to ask me about anything else?' he inquired.

'No, thank you,' said Mother suddenly. 'You have been most kind.'

I was surprised at her firmness, and then remembered that neither she nor Father had ever had any great respect for the Church. In addition, the priest represented to her the class of people who, she must have felt, had left her in the lurch when she most needed friends. She had accepted this stranger's help because she had to, but her grey eyes were steely, when she politely held out her hand to indicate dismissal.

I could see Father beginning to dither, like Bertie Wooster. He was obviously loath to let the priest go and yet was afraid that, if he said anything, Mother might start another bitter family row.

The priest settled the question by getting up abruptly. There was a hurt expression in the mild eyes. He ignored Mother's hand but inclined his head slightly towards her, as he moved through the crowded room to the door. Alan, Father and I hastened to see him out, with many protestations of gratitude. He bowed gravely, blessed us and, with slow, dignified tread, went down the steps into the darkness.

I closed the door, and stood leaning against the inside of it, while the others went back to the family. I had hoped so much that the young priest would have noticed that there were five children of school age in the family and realized that only four had been enrolled in his school. I had envisaged him instructing Father to send me with the others for lessons the following morning. But he had not noticed. I fought back my disappointment and told myself that I would probably go to school as soon as we were settled in a more permanent home, and then I would be able to play in the fresh air with new friends and perhaps even be top of the class in English once more.

The untold amount of anguish that I could have been saved if the good priest had only counted his little flock is hard to imagine. Undoubtedly, the education committee and its army of attendance officers and inspectors would have enforced my right to schooling had he but observed and reported this discrepancy.

I slunk back into the room.

'A capable man,' Mother was saying to Father, with a look which added 'unlike you'.

Before this subtle barb could be plucked out and shot back, she announced that she would go up to the bathroom. She had, hitherto, managed to use an ancient, cracked chamber-pot found under one of the beds.

Refusing Father's help with a lofty air, but using me and anything else she could to hold on to, she slowly eased her way into the hall and halfway up the narrow staircase. We sat down and rested on the stairs, and then continued. This was her first real effort to walk since her return from hospital, and she came down the stairs by going from step to step on her bottom. In spite of all the calamities she was undergoing, her strong body was healing and all that was required to return her to reasonable physical health was the will to try and strengthen her muscles. Her pretty, pink wool dress was already spoiled where the baby had wetted it, and the journey down the dusty stairs did not improve it.

The following day, she pottered round the room quite a lot, while Father went in search of that mysterious personage, 'The Parish'. The children, including Fiona, went to school and I again stayed at home. Father had made the fire and I managed to heat some water and wash Edward. When the sun came out about mid-morning, on Mother's instructions I gingerly wrapped the baby in one of the blankets.

'Take him outside and walk up and down in the sun with him,' she said.

I was gone in a flash, the startled child whimpering at my sudden movements.

The bliss of being out of the fetid room overwhelmed me, though the street was not much better. The wind, sweeping in from the estuary, was, however, invigorating despite the gas fumes carried on it. A blank brick wall shielded one side of the street, and from behind it came the shuddering sounds of shunting trains.

The house in which we were staying was one of a row of shabby, jerry-built Edwardian houses, with a grocery store at one end of the block and a public house at the other end. Toddlers with runny noses and sores on their faces scrabbled around in the gutter. An older boy, a piece of jammy bread in one hand, flitted barefoot up the road and called something insolent after me. At the door of the public house, droopy men in shabby raincoats waited for opening time. They stared at me, and I wondered why, but I must have been an unusual sight in my private school uniform, ugly velour hat rammed neatly down on to my forehead, and carrying an almost new baby up and down the pavement. School uniforms would not, in those days, have been seen in such a slummy area. I endured the silent observation with embarrassment.

A sudden diversion brought a number of women to their doors, and in some houses ragged blinds and curtains were hastily drawn.

A funeral procession came slowly down the

street, led by a gaunt man in deep black. He was followed by the hearse, a wonderful creation of black and silver, with glass side panels and small, black curtains drawn back to expose the fine wooden coffin. The coffin itself was almost covered by wreath after wreath of gorgeous flowers, including many arum lilies. The four horses which drew the hearse were well matched black carriage-horses and as they paced slowly along they tossed their heads as if to show off the long black plumes fastened to their bridles. They were driven by a coachman draped in a black cloak and wearing a top hat which shone in the sun; his face beneath the shadow of the hat looked suitably lugubrious.

The men outside the public house, with one accord, removed their caps, and the toddlers scampered out of the gutter and took refuge behind me.

The hearse was followed by a carriage in which sat a woman dressed in heavy widow's weeds. She sat well forward, so that all could see her and dabbed her purple face from time to time with a white handkerchief edged with black. Occasionally, she would bow, in a fair imitation of royalty, to one of the onlookers and then put her handkerchief again to her dry eyes. Opposite her, sat two pale, acne-pocked young men in black suits too large for them, looking thoroughly uncomfortable.

The widow's carriage was followed by five other carriages, each filled with black-clad mourners.

'Smith always does 'is funerals very nice,' said a voice behind me, rich with approval.

I glanced back quickly.

Two fat women, garbed in grubby, flowered cotton frocks, their arms tucked into their equally grubby pinafores to keep them a little warm, had come out to see the procession.

''e does. Better'n old Johnson. 'e did her daughter's wedding, too.'

There was a faint chuckle from the first woman. 'She's got more money to spend on 'er 'usband's funeral than she 'ad on the wedding, what with 'is insurance and all.' There was silence for a moment, then the voice continued, 'Ah wonder if 'er Joe will keep on the rag-and-bone business?'

Her companion murmured some reply, but I was too intrigued at the idea of a rag-and-bone man having such a large funeral procession to be interested in them further. Everybody I had seen that morning had looked so poor, and yet one of their number was being laid to rest like a prince. Surely the money such a thing would cost was needed for food.

The sun went in and my spirits drooped as the cortège turned round the corner grocery store and disappeared. Like most children, I was afraid of death and the funeral seemed an ill omen to me.

I turned, and went indoors.

Alan came home at lunch-time with a black eye. A boy had asked him if he carried a marble in his mouth, because he spoke so queerly. Alan had replied that he spoke properly, not like a half-baked savage. The half-baked savage had then blacked his eye for him.

'He's got a black eye, too,' said Alan with some satisfaction as I put a wet piece of cloth over the injured part. 'You're lucky not to have to go to this school – even the girls fight.'

'I'd like to go, just to get out of this horrid house,' I said vehemently. 'And, oh, Alan, I'm so afraid Father won't bother about sending me. You know he has always said that all a woman needed was to be able to read and write, and I can do that.'

'He'll have to send you. Isn't there a law about it?'

'Yes there is.'

'Well, the school inspector will tell him he must.'

I removed the wet cloth from his eye and cooled it again under the tap. 'If he knew I existed, I expect he would,' I agreed. 'But, Alan, I was thinking about it all night and if Father never tells them about me they will never know I am here.'

He looked at me uneasily before closing his eyes again so that I could replace the cloth over the blackened one. After wincing at my ministrations, he said doubtfully, 'Probably when we get a proper house, he'll arrange for you to go.'

'I hope so,' I responded earnestly; but I remembered the funeral and my stomach muscles were clenched with apprehension.

CHAPTER SIX

Father returned at lunch-time with food vouchers to last us for two days, while 'The Parish' made inquiries as to the rates of relief paid in the small town from which we came. Apparently, this town would have to reimburse the Liverpool public assistance committee for any relief given to us. It was expected that we would be granted forty-three shillings per week. This sum must cover everything for nine people – rent, food, clothing, heating, lighting, washing, doctor, medicines, haircuts and the thousand and one needs of a growing family.

Mother looked at him disbelievingly.

'It's impossible,' she said, her unpainted face puckered up with surprise. She was used to spending more than that on a hat.

'I can't help it,' Father said helplessly. 'That is what they told me.'

He sat, rubbing his cold hands gently together to restore the circulation, anxiety apparent in every line of him.

'I must obtain a position. But I don't even know anybody whom I could ask about a post. I have never lived in Liverpool long enough to make close friends, as you know.'

I remembered that when Mother wanted a servant she used sometimes to advertise in the newspaper, and I suggested that perhaps other posts were advertised also.

This idea was a revelation to Father and he hailed it with delight.

'By Jove, the girl is right. Look in the newspapers.'

We succeeded in borrowing the landlady's newspaper, after promising faithfully to return it intact.

And so began an endless writing of replies to advertisements on pennyworths of notepaper. Father did not know that firms frequently got seventy to eighty replies to an advertisement for a clerk, and that they just picked a few envelopes at random from the mighty pile, knowing that almost every applicant would be qualified for the post advertised.

That afternoon, Father undertook another long, cold walk, this time to the south end of the city, to look for accommodation. He had no success and returned hungry and dispirited.

Two days later 'The Parish' presented him with thirty-eight shillings, which represented forty-three shillings less five shillings for the food vouchers already supplied.

Only two more days were left of our tenancy of the rooms and our landlady had already reminded us, quite civilly, that she would require the rooms at the end of the week. Mother said, therefore, that she would take the money from 'The Parish' and, with the aid of a taxi, go to the south end of the town to see if she could find us a home.

Father protested that she was not fit for the journey, but she insisted coldly that she could manage and, after instructing me to look after baby Edward and Avril, she sent him to arrange for a taxi.

I was truly relieved to see Mother beginning to take an interest in what was to become of us, but I did not dare to tell her that my throat was ominously sore and I feared that I was getting tonsilitis again, a disease which had always plagued me.

On the advice of the taxi-driver, she alighted

in an area of tall, narrow, Victorian houses surrounding a series of squares. In the middle of each square was a communal garden which seemed to be permanently locked.

From house to house, up and down the imposing front steps, she dragged herself, knocking on doors which were cautiously opened by black, white, brown and yellow hands. Nobody would consider a family of seven children.

When she had come almost to the point of giving up, she came to a house where the door-bell actually worked. She could hear the old-fashioned clapper bell pealing in the basement. The door was answered by a tiny old lady in a long black-and-white-striped dress and a black apron. Her white hair was brushed up in Edwardian poufs and she looked very clean.

In reply to Mother's query regarding accommodation, she lifted a finger heavenward and announced piously, 'The Lord will provide!'

Mother blinked and prepared to turn away.

'Wait!' exclaimed the old lady imperiously. 'I will call Mrs Foster. Please step into the hall.'

Mother stepped in, as requested. The house was not nearly as clean as the old lady, and the lofty hall, with its peeling, olive-green wallpaper, its threadbare, dusty rug and strong smell of cooking, did not inspire confidence. An old-fashioned hatrack and an umbrella-stand made from an elephant's foot stood near the door, and behind them, set rigidly against the wall, were three Edwardian dining chairs, their woodwork lustreless and their upholstery torn.

The old lady toddled to the back of the hall and shrieked up the stairs in a strong, Liverpool accent, 'Bissis Fostaire!'

A door upstairs squeaked open and a deeper shriek replied, followed by a heavy tread on the stairs.

'God bless you, my child,' said the old lady to Mother, and vanished into what must once have been the dining-room of the house.

There was the sound of steady panting coming closer down the stairs, and Mrs Foster emerged from the gloom of the staircase.

She probably measured nearly as much round as she did in height, a veritable ball of a woman, clad in folds of black chiffon. Her neck was draped in a series of long bead necklaces, such as were worn in the nineteen-twenties, and as she moved they swayed across her bosom making rhythmical tiny clicks as they hit each other. Her pale-blue eyes had a hard, myopic stare and her double chin wobbled, as she continued to pant after reaching the hall.

Mother repeated her inquiry regarding rooms, then sat down suddenly on one of the hall chairs, and fainted.

She was aroused by the strong odour of smelling salts proffered by an old gentleman with a tobacco-stained handlebar moustache. She was vaguely aware that she was leaning against the ample bulk of Mrs Foster who was sitting in the next chair, still panting softly, like a lap-dog.

With the aid of the old gentleman and encouragement from Mrs Foster plodding up behind her, she managed to climb a double flight of stairs into what had been the drawing-room of the house, on the first floor.

The room was furnished as a bed-sitting-room. Two Cairn terriers frolicked under the high double bed; in the window stood a large cage occupied by two dismal grey parrots, and near it a cat lay on the linoleum and watched the birds with narrow, lazy eyes. The unmade bed was piled high with old clothes, and a basket table held a perilous pile of dirty dishes, while the shelf underneath it was filled with dusty ladies' magazines. A strong aroma of cats and birds permeated everything.

Mother was assisted to a chair by the cheerfully blazing fire and after a moment's hesitation the old gentleman retired, closing the door quietly after him. Mrs Foster pushed a kettle already standing on the hob round on to the fire.

'You'll feel better when you've had a cup o' tea, luv. Would you like to take off yer hat?'

Mother thankfully took off her hat and leaned back in her chair.

'That was me brother,' remarked Mrs Foster, gesturing towards the closed door. 'He has the old breakfast-room and does for himself. Me grandfather built this house.' She looked round the room proudly. 'Left it to me father, and he left it to me brother and me. We must be almost the only people left round here as owns their own house.'

She turned round and surveyed Mother, weighing her up quite accurately, as it transpired. She observed the fashionable hat, the dirty dress, the beautifully cut tweed coat, the white hands and, finally, the dead, grey face.

'Been real ill, haven't yer, luv?'

'I have, rather.'

'And you want a place for you 'n' the kids?'

'And my husband.'

'Oh, I thought mebbe he'd left you.'

'No.'

Mrs Foster silently considered this information while she assembled a tray of fine, rose-patterned crockery from a corner cupboard and made the tea.

She poured Mother a cup of tea, ladling a generous amount of sugar into it, and then sat down herself, stirring her own tea with slow, thoughtful turning of the battered spoon.

'I've got two rooms and an attic at the top of the house,' she said. 'I hadn't had in mind to have kids in them.' She paused and ran her tongue round her ill-fitting, artificial teeth. 'I had three kids there before, but they was little horrors, if you know what I mean. I don't suppose yours will be that bad.'

'They are fairly well-mannered,' Mother assured her hopefully. She sipped her over-sweet tea and its scalding heat began to revive her.

'I got two married couples and two single ladies in the rooms underneath. The married ones is at work all day, so they won't hear the noise, and the ladies – well, there's plenty like them, if they don't like it.' She put her spoon into the saucer with a decisive smack, her mind made up. 'You can have the rooms for twenty-seven shillings a week – in advance, mind you. There's a gas meter and gaslight in the kitchen-living-room.'

Mother was too thankful at having found a place for us to live in, to realize that the rent was exorbitant for such accommodation.

'Is it furnished?' Mother asked.

'Yes. There's enough furniture – and you can add a bit of your own, no doubt.'

Mother put down her cup.

'I wonder if I may see it?'

'Certainly, if you feel OK now.'

Laboriously, Mother climbed thirty-two more stairs; they were covered in ancient linoleum in which the holes threatened to trip her up from time to time.

There was a kitchen – living-room with a small bedroom fireplace. It contained a wooden table, two straight chairs, a cupboard with odds and ends of crockery and a couple of saucepans in it, a rickety, bamboo bookcase filled with dusty books and a horse-hair sofa exhibiting its intestines.

The bedroom held a black metal double bed, covered with a lumpy, stained mattress, and an ancient wardrobe with a broken door and no mirror. A further small staircase led to an attic which held another double bed. This bed lacked a leg and one corner was held up by a pile of bricks. Two trunks lay in a corner, and an old door was propped against one wall. A forgotten candlestick lay on the floor by the bed. All the floors had some linoleum on them, with dirty, wooden floor showing through in places, and all the windows were shrouded in lace curtains, grey and ragged with age.

Mother looked around her in despair.

'Nobody'd take seven children nowadays,' puffed Mrs Foster, as they descended the stairs once more.

Mother knew this to be true and, since the accommodation represented at least a roof under which to shelter, she said, 'I appreciate that, and I will take the rooms.'

They went back to Mrs Foster's room, a rent book was carefully made out and Mother paid over a week's rent. She was informed that she could hang clothes out to dry in the tiny, overgrown back garden, but the children could not play there because, to quote Mrs Foster: 'Me brother faces out back and he can't stand noise – he's a professional pianist. He used to play reelly well in a cinema.'

Mother sighed. She must have been sickened by the squalor of the place. She asked how to reach our present rooms by bus and found that a tram went from a nearby corner.

The trams were open at the front and back and the driver in a shabby uniform augmented by a huge scarf round his neck stood exposed to wind and rain, his foot for ever on his clanging bell. The conductor, not quite so well armoured against the elements, heaved young and old on and off, crammed the vehicle with loud admonitions to 'Move farther daan t' back there and make some room for them as comes atter yer', and collected the fares into his leather pouch with jingling efficiency, as he shoved and pushed his way between his close-packed passengers.

As she sat swaying in the noisy vehicle, Mother watched them work and realized that Mrs Foster had not asked if Father was employed or not; we discovered later that she had taken it for granted that he was not.

Darkness had long since fallen when Mother at last staggered into our living-room and collapsed on to the settee.

CHAPTER SEVEN

Half an hour after moving into our new abode on the following Monday, we began to appreciate some of the difficulties of living there.

Our coal was to be kept in a cupboard by the back door of the basement, where a series of old pantries had been converted for this purpose. This meant that every bucketful had to be carried up sixty-four stairs. We were to share the bathroom on the first floor with eleven other residents, and this meant innumerable trips for me up and down thirty-two stairs, since Brian, Tony and Avril were far too scared of the dark staircase and crypt-like, filthy bathroom to go down alone, and they needed help to manage in such a dirty place. I was getting resigned to disgusting bathrooms – they seemed to be part of the way of life in Liverpool, as I saw it.

The gas for the light in the living-room, and for a gas stove if we had had one to put in, came through a slot meter which ate pennies at an alarming rate. We did not know that such subsidiary meters were installed and set by landlords at the highest rate they thought they could squeeze out of their tenants. The landlords emptied these meters. They had only to pay the gas company the amount calculated on the reading of the main house meter in the basement, and they pocketed quite a substantial profit on this transaction, in addition to their rent. A more worldly-wise person than my mother would have inserted a penny and run the gas, to see how long a penny lasted, before accepting the tenancy.

Father went out and stopped a passing coal-cart, and the man brought in a sack of coal. He then went to buy cigarettes at a tiny corner store. Both he and Mother had been heavy smokers and found their enforced abstinence hard to bear.

We had brought with us on our tram journey a little oatmeal, a few potatoes, sugar and tea. There was still some baby food for Edward, and, since it was late afternoon by the time we arrived and Edward was whimpering, I made a bottle of formula and then some porridge for the other children. Alan had managed to get a smoky fire going, having lugged a handleless bucket full of coal upstairs by hugging it to his chest. His shirt, already dirty from a week's wear, was now streaked with coal dust.

Although my head was throbbing and my throat was very sore, I ate some porridge gratefully.

As there was no hot water in the bathroom, I afterwards heated pans of water on our fire, and, starting with Avril, washed all the children, except Alan, who washed himself. Little Tony, fair and silent like Fiona, felt very hot, too, and I sat him on my knee and got him back into his grubby clothes as fast as possible.

I tucked Alan, Brian and Tony up in the bed in the attic, spreading over them their three overcoats, and left them squabbling with each other regarding the fair distribution of room in the bed.

My weary mother had been resting on the bed in the bedroom, and we now held a hasty debate about where Fiona, Avril and I should sleep, it being tacitly agreed that Mother, still in pain, had to have a bed. After a long argument, Father and I brought down into the bedroom the old door which had been left in the attic. We propped this up at each corner with a pile of long-forgotten Victorian books taken from the bamboo bookcase, and then covered it with crumpled newspaper found in the wardrobe. Avril had a wonderful time chasing the spiders we dislodged from the bookcase when we took the books out. She was delighted that Fiona, she and I were going to share this improbable bed. Father and Edward would share Mother's bed.

Mother got up and went into the living-room, while I put Avril to bed, and when I joined my parents later, they were quietly muttering reproaches at each other through clouds of cigarette smoke. The problem was that we had only three shillings left from our parish relief, and we had to live, somehow, nearly three more days until Thursday afternoon when the benevolent parish would disgorge another forty-three shillings.

As I entered they broke off their recriminations and Father told me to go to bed. I went, thankfully, clinging to Fiona because I felt so dizzy. Fiona, as she took off her shoes preparatory to crawling in beside a soundly sleeping Avril, was crying silently as if her heart was already broken. Avril refused to make room for us when we pushed her gently, and grumbled drowsily that it was her bed. Desperate with the need to lie down, I slapped her legs and, with a howl and an occasional kick at her not-too-loving sisters, she made way.

With nothing over us except our overcoats, and only newspaper under us, it was unbearably cold, and yet at times I felt dreadfully hot.

After a broken night of bad dreams, through which I could hear Edward crying steadily most of the time, I staggered out of bed when Mother called me. I could hardly speak and my throat was swollen from ear to chin.

With eyes still closed she told me in a whisper to call the others, get them ready for school, cut them some bread to eat and make some milkless tea to drink.

Obediently, I built a fire and when I had fanned it with a newspaper into some semblance of heat, I put a pan of water on to it for the tea. Fiona got up from her rustling couch, leaving Avril still slumbering, and without being bidden, went downstairs to wash in the bathroom.

'The Minister's soap is nearly finished,' she reported as she brought the remains of the tablet back to me.

I went upstairs to call the boys and clung to the rickety banister because of the dizziness that enveloped me. The boys were not making their usual rumpus, and I found Alan anxiously surveying a tearful Tony, whose neck was as swollen as mine, while Brian, his small brown face looking wizened and old, was lying miserably on the mattress and saying that he didn't feel well and he wanted to go home.

'I'll tell Mother,' I said, through nearly closed lips. I noticed, in terror, that we all seemed to have very large red spots on us – mine itched abominably.

Mother looked so utterly defeated when I told her about the boys and when she had really looked at me that my heart went out to her. She woke Father, who had been sleeping the deep sleep of exhaustion.

He sat up quickly, looking very quaint in his rumpled outer clothes, and put on his spectacles.

He peered at me in an effort to persuade his slumber-ridden eyes to focus.

'I think it's mumps,' he said incredulously.

'It's my old tonsilitis,' I said in a whisper. 'My ear hurts like it always does when tonsilitis is coming.'

My voice and the room seemed to be receding from me and I burned with heat.

'I think you have mumps as well.'

'Does mumps bring you out in spots?' I asked.

He was scratching absent-mindedly at himself, as I spoke.

'Oh my God!'

He looked at his own arms, and then at my

bright red tummy, which I obligingly bared for his inspection.

'Bug bites, I think,' he said slowly. 'Saw them in the army.'

Slow tears welled into Mother's eyes.

'I can't bear it!' she cried out suddenly. 'I can't bear it!' She hammered the mattress with closed fists. 'I can't bear it!' she screamed, her pretty face distorted. 'I can't stand any more.'

She continued to shriek hysterically as we gaped at her in terrified silence. For me the scene was almost totally unreal, as fever gained on me; yet I knew that one of my parents had nearly reached the end of the amount of suffering she could accept, and it was difficult for me to contain my own screams of sheer fright.

There was the sound of heavy feet on the stairs and a coarse male voice shouted up, 'For Christ's sake, shut up up there!'

In spite of the pain it gave my throat, I began to cry.

'Don't cry, Mummy,' I begged, 'we'll get through somehow.'

Father, ever optimistic like Mr Micawber that something would turn up, bestirred himself and scrambled out of bed.

'Yes, don't cry,' he said kindly. 'I'll tell Mrs

Foster about the bugs – she'll probably do something about them.'

Having seen Mrs Foster I doubted this, but I heartily agreed. Anything, I thought, to get that desperate look off Mother's face and stop her screaming.

Slowly, as Father pottered round trying to bring some order to his distraught family, her cries gave way to sobs and she laid her head down on the mattress. She continued to weep, sobbing quietly to herself for hours.

Father trailed down to the basement to fetch some more coal and coaxed the fire into a more cheerful blaze than I had been able to create. Then we all went and stood by it while he took us one by one and looked us over.

Mother wept on, Edward and Avril slept.

In his opinion, Father said with a sigh, Tony and I had mumps. In addition, I undoubtedly had tonsilitis. Everybody was so used to my sporadic bouts of tonsilitis that this latter pronouncement did not bring me any particular sympathy. Rather, it was taken as an example of my usual awkwardness and waywardness of character. As Father said, 'You would! Just at this time.'

It was presumed that Brian was also sickening with mumps.

We three sick children were piled into the attic bed. I hardly knew, by this time, what was happening around me. Apparently, Mother was persuaded to feed Edward, when he woke, and Father fed Fiona and Alan. He then took them to their new school, where he had to part with fourpence for a week's fees.

I am not sure how my parents managed during the next few days, except that, according to Alan, they pawned my overcoat for two shillings in order to be able to buy coal. I remember, between bouts of delirium, seeing my mother crawling about, sometimes literally on her hands and knees, tears streaming down her face, as she struggled to look after Edward; and Fiona bringing me drinks of hot water with a tiny piece of Oxo cube dissolved in it.

The pain in my ears was intolerable, but there was no doctor to paint my throat with glycerine and tannin, no hot-water-bottle or aspirin to ease the searing pain, no drops in my ears to encourage a discharge. The mumps soon decreased, but it was several days before the agony in my ears suddenly diminished. There was a heavy discharge from them on to the bare mattress and my temperature began to go down. I became aware that Brian and Tony were no longer with me, and I called out, my voice seeming muffled and far away to me.

They both came clattering up the attic stairs.

Their faces seemed to have shrunk far more than the vanquished mumps justified. Brian looked more monkeylike than ever, and Tony's blue eyes and the bones of his head seemed grotesquely prominent. They both had large, scarlet spots about their faces and necks.

'It's very quiet,' I whispered. 'Where is everyone?'

'Alan and Fiona are at school. Mummy's in the living-room with the baby. We have to be quiet so she can rest.'

'That is right,' I said, trying to sit up and finding that the room swam around me, so that I was glad to lie down again. I looked imploringly at Brian. 'I'm so cold, Brian. Could you find something more to cover me with?'

He immediately went and fetched his overcoat and put it over my shoulders.

'Where is Daddy?'

'He's gone to see Mr Parish,' volunteered Tony.

I smiled at his name for the public assistance committee.

'Be a darling and bring me my specs,' I commanded him. 'I think I have to stay here a little longer. I still feel a bit hot between the shivers. Gosh, I do smell!'

The sides of my head were sticky with the discharge from my ears, but for the moment I had neither the strength nor the will to do anything about it.

'Tell Daddy I'm better, when he comes,' I said. 'You can play in here if you like.' And I closed my eyes, thankful to be free of pain at last, and fell into a deep sleep while the boys played tag up and down the room. I awoke much later to find Father bending over me, trying to see me by the light of a candlestub. He felt my head. It was cool.

'Feel better?' he asked.

'Yes.'

'That's my girl.'

'How is Mummy?'

'Much better. She is walking quite well now.'

'Has she stopped crying?' I could not keep a hint of fear out of my voice.

Father looked old and very tired, as he said quietly, 'Yes, she is better now.'

'Can I get up?'

'Yes, I think it would be a good idea. We've got a fire today, so it's warmer in the other room.'

I craved a hot cup of tea and I hoped that if we had a fire to boil the water we might also have a little tea in the cupboard. My legs almost refused to obey me and I clung to Father's arm as I shuffled across the floor, down the attic stairs and into the living-room, where I was greeted rapturously by Fiona and Alan and with a wan smile by my exhausted mother. Avril was sitting on the floor in a corner, her face red and tear-stained, getting over a tantrum.

CHAPTER EIGHT

Brian and Tony went back to school, two subdued ghosts walking hand in hand for fear of being bullied by the heavily booted older boys in the street.

Mrs Foster, declaring that she had never had a complaint before, produced half a tin of Keating's powder to repel the bugs. It did have some temporary effect, but the pests were coming in from the house next door and only a thorough stoving of both houses would ever have cleared them. We had to learn to live with them, just as we soon had to learn to live with head-lice which the children picked up in school.

I went through each child's clothing before it set off for school, hoping to save them the humiliation of being labelled verminous; they were already cowed enough.

The days dragged by and both Mother and I became stronger, despite our poor diet of white bread, potatoes and tea. Though Mother's physical health was improving, she seemed to withdraw further and further away from us. It was as if she could not bear to face the miserable existence which was our lot. She tried very hard to appear normal and calm, but attacks of hopeless hysteria descended on her without warning and she would rage and weep over some trifle, while whichever child happened to be the cause of the explosion made matters worse by trying to defend himself verbally. We were all still at the age when we believed that grown-ups knew what they were about and had sensible reasons for all that they did, and in consequence we were thrown into real fright each time one of these distressing scenes occurred. The idea that a person's life could be so shattered that they were unable to build anything new was unknown to us. We were young – we hoped for better times in the early future.

I learned to do practically everything for the baby, and when my legs were steady enough I borrowed Mother's overcoat, which though too wide was not too long for me, and took Edward and Avril down to the street for fresh air.

In Victorian times the street had been quite a

fashionable one and each house had a flight of steps up to its front door. The steps had heavy iron railings running up either side and round the area bordering the basement of the building, so that no one should fall into these tiny front yards below the level of the street.

Avril, like a squirrel released from a cage, skipped joyfully up and down the pavement, stopping occasionally to peek through the railings and catch a glimpse of someone's basement home. Her pretty blue satin bonnet, though by now rather battered, caused quite a number of favourable comments from women sitting on the steps or standing in groups gossiping. The women were mostly of the labouring class, dressing in dull greys and blacks, some with flowered pinafores and most of them wearing black shawls as protection against the cold wind. Their hair either hung in greasy confusion to their shoulders or was braided and pinned up in fashions I had seen in early Victorian photographs. Their teeth, when they smiled at Edward, were uniformly bad or non-existent. I passed them without speaking as I shyly walked up and down with Edward in my arms.

A Spanish woman was seated on the steps of the next-door house. Her greying hair was done high on her head and held at the back by a fine tortoise-shell comb and she watched my promenade with merry black eyes. Finally, she called me to her.

'Can I see your baby?' she asked in a throaty voice.

Obediently I brought Edward to her and lowered him so that she could see his sleepy face. She made delighted clucking sounds at him.

'You not have pram?' she asked.

'No.'

She looked at me carefully, weighing me up.

'Not your baby?'

'Of course he's my baby. He's my brother.'

My innocence nonplussed her for a moment. Then she laughed and pinched my cheek.

'So! He is little brother.'

'Yes. Mummy's ill,' I volunteered, warmed by her cheerfulness.

'I know. Mrs Foster tell me.'

She put her finger into Edward's hand. He promptly clutched it, and she sighed gustily.

'I got old pram. You have it. My baby big boy now. No more babies for me. You wait.'

She got up and tripped down the area steps and into the basement door under the main front steps, and I waited quietly, rocking Edward in my arms under the approving glances of her neighbours.

The best that could be said about that pram was that it had four wheels. Its lining was torn and grey with dirt; its wheels had no tyres; the ribs of its hood stood out as if it was hungry and its cover had so many cracks in it that it looked like a map of Europe. When it was moved it squeaked steadily in protest. It was, however, to be my constant companion for years and the cover had the virtue that it was firm enough to support an open book, so that I could read as I trudged along.

I was immensely grateful to my new friend and I happily laid the swaddled Edward into his new carriage. Cautiously I pulled it up the front steps of Mrs Foster's house, then up the three double flights of stairs to our room. Bumpety-bump it went on each stair and bumpety-bump went the patient Edward inside it. Mrs Foster's brother, Mr Ferris, infuriated by the regular pounding on the stairs, burst out of his room.

'For God Almighty's sake be quiet!' he shouted up. 'I can't concentrate.'

I did not answer him. I did not care about his practising on his piano. I was triumphant at having found something for Edward to sleep in and to wheel him out in.

Mother was lying down on the bed but, at the

sound of the pram's appalling squeak in the room, she sat up.

'Good heavens!' she exclaimed. 'Where did you get that ghastly chariot?'

I explained, as I took Edward out of it.

'We can't put him in a thing like that,' Mother said.

'Why not?' I asked. 'It gives him a place to sleep – you might be able to sleep better, if he wasn't in the same bed as you.'

Mother nodded acceptance, her face mirroring the hopelessness which recent events had made part of her character.

So the Chariot became part of Edward's and my life and squeaked its way painfully through miles and miles of black Liverpool streets. Sometimes I think there must still be two little ghosts and a squeak floating gently through Princes Park because we went there so often.

CHAPTER NINE

Mother still had in the stitches from the major operation which had been performed upon her soon after Edward's birth. I had seen the scarifying gash which ran from above her waist to her pelvis; it was now healed and should really have been examined by a surgeon some time back. We considered getting the stitches out ourselves, but we had no scissors and Father was afraid to risk cutting them with his blunt razor. It was decided, therefore, that next time Father drew our allowance from the public assistance committee, Mother would have to see a doctor, no matter what we had to go without as a result of having to pay his fee.

Two mysterious middle-aged ladies, who went out only in the evening, and two married couples lived on the floor below us. With strict instructions from Father not to speak to either of the single ladies, who were, I was assured, not 'nice', I was dispatched to inquire from one of the married couples the name of a doctor.

A man in mechanic's overalls answered my knock. He was undersized and very thin, his hair slicked back from a long, narrow face. Tired, hazel eyes regarded me kindly.

'What do you want, luv?'

'My father sent me down to ask if you know where we could find a doctor round here.'

'Soombody took ill, luv?' His voice was much more alert.

'No, thank you. Mummy was very ill before we came here and now she must see a doctor – to have her stitches removed.'

'Oh, ay. Just a minute, ducks, I'll ask the wife.'

He left me standing at the open door, while he retreated into the room. I caught a glimpse of a stoutish blonde girl ladling stew out of a saucepan on to plates at a table by the window. The room was crowded with a bed, a stove and living-room furniture, but the general effect was of cosy friendliness. The smell of the stew was unbelievably good and I sniffed appreciatively as I waited.

The girl put down the saucepan and they both came to the door. She wiped her hands on a grubby apron as she looked down at me.

'There's the parish doctor,' she said doubtfully. 'But none of us goes to 'im unless we're dying. Tell yer Dad that Dr Dent around the corner by the grocery shop is proper kind. He wouldn't charge you much – but you'd better take half a crown, in case.'

I thanked her and was just about to turn and run back upstairs, when she put her hand in her pocket and brought out a toffee. ''Ere yer are, luv. Have a toffee.'

I had not tasted a sweet since I had arrived in Liverpool and I accepted the gift delightedly and rushed up the stairs with unseemly exuberance.

''is surgery hours are seven to nine,' she called up after me.

Father normally went to the library in the evening to read the *Liverpool Echo* and write replies to any advertisements which offered office jobs, so I was told to accompany Mother to the doctor's surgery. Alan would take care of the rest of the family while we were away.

Mother washed herself as best she could with a piece of rag dipped into cold water, and made sure she had no vermin on her. I did the same and also combed my hair; we had only one small pocket comb between us and were always afraid of breaking it, as we could not afford to replace it; consequently, I hardly ever combed my straggling locks. Since my overcoat was still in pawn, I borrowed Fiona's.

For the first time since she had arrived, Mother made the long trip downstairs. The night was clear and frosty and she paused at the top of the front steps to take a big breath of fresh air; it smelled good after the foul atmosphere of the house. Slowly we proceeded down the steps and down the street, to a cross street of smaller houses and shops. We found the doctor's front door, which led straight off the street, except for two small steps. A notice on the door invited us to enter. I turned the well-polished brass handle, it gave, and we went in.

We found ourselves in a narrow hall in which ancient brown linoleum gleamed with much polishing under a low-watt light. To our right was a door slightly ajar, marked 'Waiting-Room'. This proved to be packed with people, many of them Negroes, sitting on chairs ranged round the walls of the room; the centre was occupied by a large Victorian dining-table on which a number of tattered magazines lay in disarray. A gas fire, turned low, stood in front of a black, iron fireplace. On the varnished mantelpiece a marble clock ticked despondently, while on either side of it two cast-iron Greek warriors kept guard.

A whisper of conversation ceased as we entered and all eyes regarded us. I suppose that Mother's pale pink hat caused the interest. While we hesitated, a huge man in an old macintosh got up off his chair and offered it to Mother, who, by this time, was looking very white.

'Thank you,' she said and sat down gratefully.

The man grinned sheepishly, his great red face breaking into a thousand wrinkles, as he stood near us fingering a greasy cap. I stood close to Mother, feeling a little frightened. This was all so different from the chintz-clad sitting-room of our old doctor and the ready welcome of his smart little wife.

Neither of us had any idea how one communicated the fact of one's presence to the doctor. But we soon saw that at the other end of the room was another door and that at the sound of a buzzer people went in and out of it. Presumably the doctor was in the next room. We could not guess how people established when they could go in so we sat and sat until we were the last people in the waiting-room, and the front door was closed and locked by an elderly woman. When the buzzer rang again, Mother rose and went in to see the doctor, and I was left alone.

I got up and went to stand by the gas fire. The unaccustomed warmth was delicious and wrapped itself around me in a comfortable blanket of heat. I gazed at the iron Greek soldiers on the mantelpiece and smiled at them. My grandmother had such a pair on her kitchen mantelpiece in her beautiful little house on the other side of the Mersey. The tears sprang to my eyes as I remembered it. How long would it be, I wondered, before I had twopence so that I could take the ferry across the Mersey and visit her. My parents never mentioned her and she did not write to me. Probably she did not even know where I was. I wondered if I dare write to her without my parents' permission. Impatiently I wiped away the tears. Paper and stamps cost money, too, you stupid, I told myself.

The doctor was taking a long time over Mother's stitches. Perhaps he would make her quite well. Then she could look after the children and I could go back to school. Perhaps in school there would be a school-teacher who would tell me what steps one had to take to get work when one had finished school.

I had always wanted to be a ballet-dancer and my father had indulged me in this by sending me to a very good teacher when I was about five years old. Just before my seventh birthday, however, a very heavy, old-fashioned wardrobe had unexpectedly fallen over while I was in my parents' bedroom, catching my legs under it. This had resulted in one of my feet being permanently slightly twisted. It was not an unsightly crippling but was sufficient to make any dancing career impossible. During the months I had had to lie with the foot up I had discovered a natural ability for drawing, and this had led to an ambition to design clothes for the theatre.

I gazed into the doctor's miserable gas fire and saw gorgeous imaginary figures in clothes designed by me tripping and leaping across an imaginary stage. I wished I had a pencil and paper to catch and record permanently my pretty dream. If only the doctor would make Mother well, I would study and draw and practise and fill the stage of the Liverpool Empire with such glamour as its old walls had never seen before.

There was a click as the doctor opened his surgery door for Mother and bowed her out, and she smiled her delicate, beguiling smile at him.

He was a dark, intense-looking young man; he was, I later discovered, an ardent communist who tried his best to practise his beliefs in the stinking slum in which we lived. He grinned cheerfully at me and said good night to us both.

'What did he say?' I asked anxiously as I held Mother's arm to steady her, after the doctor's housekeeper had locked the front door behind us.

We walked slowly down the empty street for a little way before Mother answered.

'He said I should have gone to the outpatients department of a hospital.'

'Did he take the stitches out? Did it hurt?'

'Yes, he took them out – it didn't hurt much – he's a surgeon as well as a physician.'

In a trembling voice I asked another question, one with selfish intent. Behind it was my despair at the drudgery I was facing and my hopes that if I was allowed to go to school I might find a way out from being for ever the unpaid, unthanked housekeeper for our poverty-stricken family.

'Will you be all right?' I asked. 'Will you get better?'

'He thinks I will, if I go to work – in the open air.'

'Work?' I was truly astonished.

At my query she looked down at me, but there was no affection, no real interest in her gaze or in her voice as she answered, 'Yes. Work.'

The idea that work could cure someone who had been ill was too difficult for me to understand. I knew nothing of mental illness, except that lunatics were shut up in lunatic asylums, and I had no comprehension of the mental stress under which my poor mother laboured and which the doctor had diagnosed.

'You can't,' I said desperately. 'There is Edward – and Avril – and me – I haven't got my matric yet – I have to go back to school.'

'We shall see,' she said thoughtfully.

My stomach clenched in a deadly nervous pain. In a perceptive flash I saw myself for ever at home, the uneducated daughter retained to help in the house – and there were still some of these when I was a child – grey, uninteresting, the butt of everyone's ill-temper, without money of my own and consequently entirely dependent upon the goodwill of the rest of the family. I saw myself for ever struggling with the care of Edward, with Avril's tantrums and the boys' fights, with Mr Parish's miserable pittance, and I realized that the daughter who did not have to go to school or to work would be the one to be clothed and fed last.

I burst into tears, my hopes shattered.

'Oh no, Mummy!' I wailed. 'I want to go to school! I want to be like other girls!'

'Be quiet,' said Mother sharply. 'You are making an exhibition of yourself.'

I continued to weep – but quietly. Little ladies did not make exhibitions of themselves in public.

'You have to learn that you cannot have everything you want. The family must come first.'

CHAPTER TEN

Immediately we arrived home, I threw a tantrum which left even Avril awed. I stamped, I cried, I shouted that I would go to school. Twelve and a half was too young an age to have to leave. I would not stay at home and look after babies.

My bewildered father, who did not know what the cause of my rage was, shouted at me above the storm to be quiet. Mother shouted back at him. Fiona and Tony, terrified by the noise, wept steadily in a corner, while Alan did his best to placate the various contestants by telling everyone to shut up. Brian took refuge halfway up the attic stairs and watched through the banister. Baby Edward cried for his forgotten bottle. A voice from below yelled up to us, 'Shut that bloody racket, can't yer!'

As my anger gave way to hopeless tears Father gradually picked up the story and said he thought the doctor's idea of Mother's going to work was an excellent one and that it would probably be for only a little while. When I continued to weep passionately, he slapped me across the buttocks and told me to go into the bedroom until I could behave in a civilized manner.

I lay face down on the bed until I could not stand the stench of it any more. The nervous strain under which the children laboured in their cold, hungry, new world was so great that Brian, Tony and Avril had become incontinent at night and Edward had no rubber undersheet to help him, so that the already disgusting beds had become even more so and were invariably wet somewhere on their surface.

Emerging finally in sulky silence and with blood-shot eyes, I found Edward still whimpering disconsolately, but the children were silently getting themselves ready for bed, by taking off their outer clothes. My parents were arguing heatedly about what kind of occupation my Mother could undertake.

Still sniffing, I made a bottle for Edward with the last of the baby food, and, since I was still filled with resentment at my parents, I took him outside and sat down on the top stair of the long flights of gloomy staircase and fed him.

The smell of the overcrowded, verminous house, its filthy, over-used bathroom and the efforts of nine different cooks combined with Edward's rancid odour was almost overpowering, and I put my cheek against his scurvy little head and wept again.

During the next few days my mother went out each afternoon for a walk to strengthen her legs, and then one day she sponged her dress and pressed it with an iron borrowed from Miss Sinford, the benevolent, crazy old lady on the ground floor, wiped her shoes over with a wet cloth, and washed herself down with a rag and cold water. She then made up her face with the last of her make-up and the aid of her handbag mirror, and went out without saying where she was going.

As she went down the stairs, I realized for the first time how much my mother had changed. She had been considered beautiful and extremely vivacious and had always had a court of young men who called upon her – there were still some gentlemen who lived on private incomes in those days and who had time to call and take tea with a pretty woman and her friends – but now her dress hung loosely on her, her face was haggard and lined, her shining black hair, which had been exquisitely kept by her hairdresser, had grown long and straggling; she had pushed it up under her hat before going out. The polished ovals of her nails were ruined by her having to bite them to shorten them, as we all had to do, because we had no scissors. How much had Father changed, I wondered? And the children? And me?

Avril was howling because she could not go out too, and I decided that I might create a diversion by washing her and washing Edward.

We had a fire that day, a luxury we frequently had to forgo despite the icy February weather, so I went down to the bathroom with our kettle and only saucepan, filled them with water, brought them upstairs and set them on the fire. Carrying Edward on my hip, I took the handleless coal bucket down to the basement area, a stone-lined yard from which steps led up to the back garden. I laid Edward on a counter which must have been part of a butler's pantry in the more palmy days of the house, and washed the coal dust out of the bucket as thoroughly as I could under a tap in the yard.

Watched by a fascinated Avril, who had by now forgotten her desire to go out and had tripped up and downstairs behind me puffing excitedly, I set the bucket in front of the fire, put the warm water in it, stripped a protesting Edward and washed him from head to heel, holding him on my knee as I had seen my nanny hold Avril when she was a baby. This was the first time he had had a complete bath since we had left home and I found that he had numerous bug bites and his little back was sore where the urine had not been properly washed off him; his head was covered with scurf.

I had no change of clothing for him, but I pinned a piece of the rag the priest had given us on him as a rough diaper and laid his blanket over him to keep him warm in the Chariot while I dealt with Avril.

Fortunately, Avril thought it was a wonderful game and submitted to being rubbed all over with a wet cloth. I could not wash her head because I could not think how to do it in a bucket. Dirt was ingrained in her skin and I could not get her completely clean without soap. I had an uneasy feeling that her fine golden hair was verminous and certainly she had scurf around her forehead and along the line of the parting. It seemed, too, as if the hair on the crown of her head was thinner than before. I told her cheerfully, however, that I would wash her vest and knickers after she was in bed.

I sighed as I slicked the water off her in front of the fire, so that she would dry quickly. She, like Mother, had changed. She had been a pudgy child with rosy cheeks; now she looked wan, her ribs showed and her stomach stuck out too much.

While I scrubbed the children, Father was stuck in one of his everlasting queues.

He worked very hard at being unemployed. He spent most of two days a week walking to the employment exchange, standing in a long queue, signing on as being available for work and walking back up the hill which was Leece Street, pausing outside the old Philharmonic Hall to read the concert notices with wistful attention, then on past the black-faced ear, nose and throat hospital and then through an endless maze of decaying Victorian houses to our comfortless eyrie at the top of one of them. He was not so badly off as dock labourers, he told us. They had to sign on for work twice a day.

Another day was spent walking to the offices of the public assistance committee, where could be found Tony's 'Mr Parish'. Here he stood in a long queue again, soaked by rain or frozen in the winter wind, and received his precious forty-three shillings a week. He then walked home. On the other three mornings a week he went to the public library, scanned the advertisements in the newspapers in the reading-room, and wrote replies to those offering work he felt he could do. Then he walked all the way into the centre of the town to deliver his replies to the offices of the *Liverpool Echo* in Victoria Street, because we had no money for stamps – the postage for a letter in those days was three-halfpence.

His shoes wore through at the soles and he stuffed them with cardboard begged from the corner grocery shop, until the holes were so big that the cardboard would not stay in place. Without tools he could not hope to mend them himself, so one week we very nearly starved completely while we paid the shoemaker. He had not had a haircut or a clean shirt for a month, though he had managed to wash himself quite thoroughly. His socks had very little left from the ankle down, and I remember his blue, frozen feet sticking out of them when he removed his soaking wet shoes on his return in the evenings. I think it was rubbing his feet with my hands which truly brought home to me our desperate position and made me accept the fact that I had to stay at home. I would rub until I had the circulation going again and he would whistle under his breath with the pain of it, and each time it happened my heart broke anew.

For a month or more, he never spoke to anyone outside the family, except the city and government clerks who dealt with him and to whom he was just another statistic. One morning, however, the wait at the employment exchange was particularly long and chilly, and the ragged queue of weary men began to mutter rebelliously, and Father was drawn into sympathetic conversation with his fellow sufferers. They were, for the most part, respectable working men many of whose jobs were dependent upon the ships which went in and out of the port of Liverpool in normal times. They were curious about my father, because he spoke like an educated man. They could not imagine that anyone highly educated could be unemployed; they assumed, and Father did not disillusion them, that he had been a senior clerk in one of the shipping companies which had been dispensing with its office staff. They were friendly and, as Father met them again and again, they began to fill him in on how to stay alive under almost impossible circumstances.

He discovered that many of them had wives who went out cleaning private homes or worked in stores to augment their parish relief; though these earnings should have been declared to the public assistance committee, they were not, and they made all the difference between starvation and dying more slowly of malnutrition.

'If you can live long enough, there just might be a job for you one morning,' a leather-faced old warehouseman told him jokingly.

There were agencies in the town, he was told, which would provide the odd pair of shoes or an old blanket for a child. There were regimental funds willing to provide a little help to old soldiers. He gathered other scraps of information, which were revelations to a man who had never had to think twice about the basic necessities of life. An open fire, he was assured, could be kept going almost all day from the refuse of the streets, old shoes, scraps of paper, twigs, wooden boxes, potato peelings; if one was very ill or had a broken bone, the outpatients departments of most of the local hospitals would give some medical care. Pawnbrokers would take almost anything saleable, and one could buy second-hand clothing from them. Junk yards would sometimes yield a much needed pram wheel or a piece for an old bike. One could travel from Liverpool to London by tramcar, if one knew the route, and it was much cheaper than going by train. Some of the men had done it several times in an effort to find work in the more prosperous south-east of the country.

Father thanked them gratefully and came home very thoughtful, marvelling at their sheer resilience and good nature in such adversity.

All of us had colds, including the baby, and lacked even handkerchiefs, though we did our best by using newspaper culled from the greengrocer, who wrapped our small purchases of potatoes in it. Father began to realize that unless help came quickly the younger children would probably die from the first germ that infected them. The death rate in Liverpool, at that time, was one of the highest in the country and the infant mortality rate was correspondingly horrifying. He knew that we were worse off than most of the people who stood in the endless queues with him, since we did not draw the Liverpool level of relief, nor were we eligible for help with clothing which 'Mr Parish' sometimes gave out. No one, in all his conversations, happened to tell him that he was paying three times the rent that most people paid and that this was largely what was crippling us.

By far the greatest proportion of the Liverpool work-force was casual labour, dependent upon the erratic comings and goings of ships in the river, and most men were accustomed to being unemployed from time to time, particularly dock labourers. Their pattern of life reflected this in that they could never make a proper domestic budget, because they never knew from one week to the next what their earnings would be. They spent their earnings and 'made do' in between jobs. My father, being an educated man trained to study economic trends, could never manage to be as philosophical and optimistic as they were. He feared not only for himself but for his children's future.

In those days there were no midday meals or drinks of milk at school to help children along. One good lady who suggested that the skimmed milk thrown down the drain by one of the city's bigger dairies might be given free to children in the elementary schools was soundly snubbed for her socialistic ideas.

Father swallowed what little pride he had left. He sat down at our greasy table and wrote to the headquarters of his old regiment.

Mother came home white with weariness and irritable with frustration, having tried unsuccessfully against about thirty other applicants for a job as a saleswoman.

'They looked like a flock of crows,' she remarked of the applicants. 'They all wore black dresses, stockings and shoes – just little white collars to relieve the dreariness.'

'I thought that was what shop-girls always wore,' replied Father.

'I suppose so,' Mother said. She added, 'And the hours one was expected to work – nine until nine on Saturdays!'

'What wages were they offering?'

'Fifteen shillings a week.'

Father whistled. 'That's not a living wage,' he said.

'They don't care,' replied Mother wearily. 'All the women there were anxious to get the job.'

CHAPTER ELEVEN

Each day my mother went out to try and get work and spent most of the morning and afternoon in a fruitless round of offices and shops. Before leaving, she would give me a shilling to buy the day's food. This I laid out to the best of my ability on bread, potatoes, rice, tea, sugar, pennyworths of bacon scraps or margarine and, that dire necessity, a pint of milk for Edward, which cost twopence.

At first, Edward used to cry with hunger, but as he grew a little older, he would lie lethargically in the Chariot, making no sound most of the time. The other children also grew apathetic and the smaller ones tried to take bits of bread when I was not looking. We never heard from the school about their progress nor did my father inquire.

One morning my parents went out quite early,

before Edward had been fed. After the children had been given a meagre bowl of porridge each and had been sent to school, there was no food left in the house. I was desperate with hunger. And the usual pint of milk would, I knew, not be enough to last Edward for twenty-four hours. However, clutching the shilling, I wrapped Edward up in his stinking blanket, put on my woollen cardigan, my coat being still in pawn, and went downstairs to buy milk from the first passing milkman.

Standing on the doorstep were two pint bottles of milk, presumably delivered for Miss Sinford, the lady with religious mania, and Mrs Hicks, who lived with her unemployed husband in the bowels of the basement. The other tenants patronized a milkman who came later.

I looked at the bottles and then up and down the apparently empty street, hoping that the milkman might still be near by. There was no sign of him, however, and I turned back into the house with the idea of getting out the Chariot and wheeling it round to the dairy to purchase Edward's precious pint.

Edward began to whimper. I looked down longingly at the milk bottles. Then, like a fleeing cat, I tore up the stairs, Edward bobbing up and down in my arms. I laid him down gently in the Chariot, took our two cracked cups, ran down to the bathroom and filled one with water, then ran silently down the rest of the stairs to the front door.

I glanced quickly up and down the street. Everyone was apparently sleeping the long hopeless sleep of the unemployed.

Quickly I took the lids off the bottles, filled the empty cup with a little milk from each bottle, topped the bottles up with water, carefully replaced the lids, shook the bottles gently, and then crept upstairs again with my precious prize.

I managed to make a feed for Edward before the little fire I made from paper flickered out, and I fed him contentedly, knowing that I could make the pint of milk I would buy stretch further for him. I had no qualms of conscience about my theft – I thought only of Edward – and I was mercifully unaware that the policeman on the beat had quietly watched the whole operation.

It was late February, with days of pouring rain interspersed with weak sunshine. The trees and bushes in the locked gardens in the squares were beginning to show a faint swelling of their buds, and, as I wheeled Edward to the tiny local grocery shop and to the greengrocer's each day, I would wonder why the children running in and out of the traffic or playing with cigarette cards on the pavement could not be allowed to play in the gardens. I would stand watching them dully as they cursed and tumbled each other about, their white or black skins equally grey with dirt and dust, their noses dribbling, their bare legs chapped and with septic sores on their knees. Little girls would play endless games of skipping and hopscotch, each with its appropriate song, learned from their elder sisters and passed down from generation to generation.

'I am a girl guide dressed i' blue,
These are the actions I must do.
Salute to the King, bow to the Queen
And turn my back to the people.
Pepper!'

And at the word 'pepper' they would turn the skipping-rope with feverish speed to see how many fast skips they could do before being tripped up. Sometimes, I would wish wistfully that I might be able to join in, but I had always to watch Avril and Edward and I was mortally afraid of something happening to them in this strange world which I did not understand.

Another pleasure was to stand in front of the greengrocer's and contemplate the neat pyramids of oranges, apples, lemons and tomatoes. Mentally, I ate my way through the piles from top to bottom. I lacked the courage and initiative of the little street arabs, who would sometimes snatch a piece of fruit and fly like jets down the narrow back alleys, there to consume it with much ribaldry at the expense of the outraged greengrocer. A cry of 'Bobby' or 'Cop' or 'Flattie' would, however, send them speeding off again, old gym shoes or bare feet thudding over the flagstones like rapidly bouncing rubber balls.

With Edward replete with Miss Sinford's and Mrs Hick's milk and sleeping quietly in the Chariot, Avril and I went on the usual shopping round. At the greengrocer's I stood and dithered. If I bought rice, I argued with myself, Mother would say that I should have bought potatoes; if potatoes, then she would say rice. I knew I could not win. Mother was getting better and her increasing irritability at my sins was a sign of it.

The policeman on his beat stopped and chucked Edward under his chin. Edward opened his eyes and managed a small smile. I looked up and smiled too, my morning peccadillo completely forgotten.

'Nice baby you've got,' he said, putting his hands behind his back and rocking gently on his heels.

He beamed at me from under his helmet. 'What's his name?'

'Edward,' I said. He was a nice-looking young man, neat and clean, despite the acne spots all over his face.

'And what's your name?'

'Helen,' I replied promptly.

He looked down at the baby again, while the greengrocer peered through the glass of his window, which he had been polishing.

'No Mummy?'

'Yes, she's looking for work. So's Daddy.'

He looked surprised, apparently at my clear English, so different from that of the other children round about. It was better English than he spoke himself.

'Having a hard time? Got any other brothers and sisters?'

'Yes,' I said simply, in answer to the first question. 'We are seven. The others are all at school.'

The wind was getting up and it was beginning to rain. My teeth started to chatter and I wrapped my cardigan closer round me.

The policeman stared at me with calm blue eyes and said, 'Humph.' He adjusted the collar of his cape. I became aware of the interested gaze of the greengrocer, and decided on rice for supper.

'Goodbye,' I said to the policeman and pushed the pram a bit farther along the street and parked it outside the grocery shop, where Avril watched it while I went inside. The policeman, after a moment's hesitation, went into the greengrocer's shop.

The following morning a pint of milk was delivered to the top landing of our staircase. When I ran downstairs to catch the milkman and return the bottle to him, he insisted that it was for Edward and was sent by a friend, and not even Father could make him say any more. For two long intolerable years the milkman stolidly climbed the stairs and deposited a pint of milk on our top step. It probably saved Edward's life.

Many years later, the greengrocer told my mother about the young policeman who had inquired about us from him, and had then gone round to the dairy and ordered a daily pint of milk to be delivered for Edward, and had paid for it out of his own meagre wages.

CHAPTER TWELVE

One of the advantages of being very poor is that one has time. Since we had no clothes except those on our backs, there was no pile of washing to be dealt with each Monday. When there is little food, there is little cooking, and since we possessed no bed linen, towels, cleaning materials or tools, most other domestic jobs either were non-existent or could not be carried out. As the weather improved, therefore, I began to take a walk each day, pushing Edward and Avril in the Chariot.

These were, for me, voyages of discovery into a world I had never dreamed of before. I meandered along narrow streets, where the soot-blackened early Victorian houses opened directly upon the pavement. Some of the houses had the flagstone across their front door scrubbed and neatly whitened, with a strip of well-shone brass covering the sill; their painted window-sills were carefully polished and their garish chintz curtains were starched as stiff as the sentries outside Buckingham Palace. Others were like our house: dull windows veiled in grey webs of lace, window-panes missing and filled in with cardboard, old orange-peel and cigarette-ends littering their frontage.

The local pawnbroker's shop, with its dusty sign of three golden balls hanging outside over a wooden table piled high with second-hand clothing, made for me a fascinating treat. I loved to gaze in the windows at the rows of Victorian and Edwardian rings for sale, the war medals, violins, blankets, china ornaments and sailors' lucky gold charms.

The pawnbroker himself was part of the scene, as he stood in his doorway puffing at a cigarette, shirt-sleeves rolled up to show olive-coloured arms, tight black curls receding from his forehead, a magnificent watch-chain with dangling seals swathed across a wrinkled, blue serge waistcoat over a comfortable paunch.

'Come on, me little blue-eyed duck!' he would call to Avril when he saw her, and occasionally he would feel around in his waistcoat pocket with his tobacco-stained fingers to dig out a grubby sweet for her. She loved him and would howl dismally on the days when we did not walk that way. For me, he would have a polite nod and a brief 'Afternoon. Nice day', regardless of whether it rained or shone.

One mild March afternoon, I circled the cathedral and listened to the ring of the stonemasons' tools on its great sandstone walls. It rose like a graceful queen above slums which put Christianity to shame. I stared up the beautiful sweep of steps leading to its entrance, wondering if I dare go in, but I was too afraid. I had not seen myself in a mirror since coming to Liverpool, but I knew I was both dirty and shabby. My hat and shoes had been passed to Fiona, who was obliged to go out to school, whereas I could stay indoors. The shoes had been replaced by a pair of second-hand running shoes with holes in the toes; my head was bare and my hair straggled in an unruly mass down my neck; it was rarely combed and never washed.

Still pushing aimlessly, I wandered along Rodney Street, a lovely street of well-kept Georgian houses, the homes and surgeries of Liverpool's more eminent doctors. A brass plaque on No. 62 informed me that Gladstone was born there. Mr Gladstone was not one of my heroes, so I continued onward enjoying the peace and orderliness of the quiet road.

I turned down Leece Street, past the employment exchange where Father spent so many unhappy hours, past tall, black St Luke's Church and into Bold Street, the most elegant shopping centre in Liverpool. Although there were at least a dozen empty shops up for rent, the atmosphere was one of opulence. I pushed past women in fur coats and pretty hats, who stared at me in disgust, to look in windows which held a single dress or fur or a few discreet bottles of perfume. A delicious odour of roasting coffee permeated the place.

Onward I went, through the packed shopping area of Church Street, where trams, nose to tail, clanged their way amid horsedrawn drays, delivery vans and private cars, and newspaper men shouted to me to 'read all abaat it'. The cry of '*Echo, Echo, Liverpool Echo,* sir' comes wafting down the years, like the overwhelming scent of vanilla pods, the sound and smell of a great port.

'I know where we'll go,' I said to Avril, who was bouncing up and down in the Chariot pretending it was a horse.

'Where?'

'We'll go down to the Pier Head!'

I knew this part of the town, because I had

been shopping in it on many occasions with my grandmother. I pushed the Chariot purposefully up Lord Street to the top of the hill, where Queen Victoria in pigeon-dropped grey stone presided, down the hill, through a district of shipping offices with noble names upon their doors: Cunard, White Star, Union Castle, Pacific & Orient, the fine strands which tied Liverpool to the whole world. Past the end of the Goree Piazzas, an arcade of tiny shops and offices, where out-of-work sailors lounged and spat tobacco and called hopefully after me, under the overhead railway which served to take the dockers to work, and a last wild run across the Pier Head, dodging trams and taxis, to the entrance to the floating dock.

At last I had found it!

The river scintillated in the sunshine; a row of ships was coming in on the tide; a ferry-boat and a pilot-boat tethered to the landing-stage rocked rhythmically; screeching gulls circled overhead and swooped occasionally to snatch food from the river. A cold wind from the sea tore at my cardigan, jostling and buffeting my skinny frame. I put the hood of the Chariot up to shield Avril and Edward from it.

The shore hands were casting off the ferry-boat, and I looked wistfully out across the water at the empty Cammell Laird shipyards in Birkenhead. My eyes followed the shore along to the spires of Wallasey, and mentally I followed the railway with all its dear familiar station names along the coast to West Kirby. On that railway-line lived Grandma, who was so angry with Father that she never wrote to us. There was a middle-class world, where people could still wash every day in clean bathrooms. The slump had reached some of them, I guessed; but once past Birkenhead, I thought sadly, it could not be half as miserable as Liverpool was. Perhaps, if I could see Grandma and describe to her my mother's terrible suffering and my father's despair, she would forgive them and help them.

I longed to push the Chariot up the ramp of the ferry-boat and escape, run away from our smelly rooms, from hunger and cold, the cold which was raking through me mercilessly now, and from people who looked like the gargoyles on the old cathedrals I had attended in the past.

'The ferry costs twopence,' I reminded myself, as I wrapped Avril and Edward closer in their inadequate piece of blanket, 'and you haven't got twopence.' Furthermore, Grandma, though long since widowed, had been married to a businessman who never failed, and who had come from a long line of ironmasters and merchants who always seemed to have done very well for themselves – she just would not understand.

The way home seemed incredibly long, and I paused at the bottom of Bold Street, to stand for a moment in the warmth of a shop doorway before continuing. A shopwalker behind the glass door frowned at me as I hauled the Chariot close in. The shoppers were thinning out rapidly and I watched them hurrying to their cars, parked at the kerb, or into Central Station. And there she was!

Joan! My own best friend!

She was sauntering down the pavement in her neat school uniform, her mother beside her, presumably here on one of her visits to her grandmother. I had not seen her since leaving my old home and, presumably, she knew nothing of my recent adventures – one day I had attended school with her; the next day I had been whisked away to Liverpool.

I started forward.

'Joan!' I cried, my heart so full of gladness I thought that I would burst with sheer joy. 'Oh, Joan!'

The mother stopped, as did Joan. The smiles which had begun to curve on their lips died half born. Without a word, they both wheeled towards the road, crossed it and disappeared into Central Station.

I stared after them dumbly. They *had* recognized me. I knew they had. Then why had they not stopped and spoken to me?

A gentleman told me irritably to get out of the way and I became aware that the Chariot and I were blocking the pavement. Still dumbfounded, I turned the pram homeward and slowly pushed it up the hill, gazing vacantly before me.

Coming towards me, amid the well-dressed shoppers, was an apparition. A very thin thing draped in an indescribably dirty woollen garment which flapped hopelessly, hair which hung in rat's tails over a wraithlike grey face, thin legs partially encased in black stockings torn at the knees and gaping at the thighs, flapping, broken canvas covering the feet. This thing was attached to another one which rolled drunkenly along on four bent wheels; it had a torn hood through which metal ribs poked rakishly.

I slowed down nervously, and then stared with dawning horror.

I was looking at myself in a dress-shop window.

It was a moment of terrifying revelation and I started to run away from myself, pushing the pram recklessly through groups of irate pedestrians, nearly running down a neatly gaitered bishop. Every instinct demanded that I run away and hide, and for a few minutes my feet were winged. Halfway up the hill, back in the shadow of St Luke's, however, under-nourishment had its say, and I sank exhausted on the church steps, while Avril giggled contentedly in the pram after her rapid transit up the street.

I was disgusted with myself. I felt I could have done more. I was old enough to know that I should wash myself; at least cold water was available. And if I could wash garments through for the children, I could have put some of my own through the same water. I realized, with some astonishment, that I had always been told what to do. The lives of all the children had until recently been strictly regulated by a whole heirachy of domestics, some of them very heavy-handed, and a father who had, at times, used a cane with sharp effect. I washed when told to wash, went to school when told to go, however irksome it seemed, got out my playthings when permission was given. Disobedience was a crime and to query or object to adult orders, which were given without any supporting explanation or reason for them, was quite unthinkable. I don't think that I had ever had an original thought until I had been plunged into this queer life in Liverpool, where I had been given the job of looking after my brothers and sisters.

Now, sitting on the blackened stone steps of the soaring Gothic church, I realized that neither Father nor Mother nor Grandmother nor servant was particularly interested in me. With all the bitterness and unreasonableness of a budding teenager, I saw myself as a convenient tool of my parents, my only reason for existence that I could take the care of the children off them.

I fastened the two remaining buttons of my cardigan, got up and wheeled the Chariot slowly up Upper Duke Street, skirting St James Cemetery with some trepidation in the gathering gloom. For the first time, I tried to think constructively, to devise ways in which the family might get out of the morass in which it was floundering; but my experience was too limited and my mind too dulled by lack of use, my body by lack of food, for me to be able to come up with a possible solution. Greater minds than mine were having trouble with the same problem. We were but one family amid millions of others.

I cried openly as I trudged along, my glasses sliding slowly down my nose, the tears making white rivers in my grey face.

When my parents came in that evening, I again

brought up the question of my going to school. I was always very nervous when trying to communicate with them and probably I mentioned the subject too diffidently, because when I suggested that I would have to complete my education before I could hope to go to work in the future, Mother simply dismissed me by saying, 'Don't be absurd. Go and put Avril to bed.' Father laughed and added, 'I hope no daughter of mine will ever have to go to work.'

Father's kindly meant remark startled me. Even a young girl like myself knew that times were changing and more and more women were entering the labour force. Lancashire had, in addition, a long tradition of women working, and the only future I could visualize as holding an iota of happiness for myself was one which contained a career.

'But . . .' I began.

'That is enough, Helen. Do as you are told.'

And Helen, being a coward, did as she was told.

CHAPTER THIRTEEN

With the exception of a weekly visit from an officer of the public assistance committee, which consisted of a quick counting of heads and a few questions snapped at my parents, we had no visitors. I was, therefore, surprised when I arrived home from one of my visits to the Pier Head to find a well-dressed gentleman standing at the door, asking Miss Sinford where he could find my father.

I waved at Alan, who was shepherding the other children along the road, and went up the steps backwards pulling the Chariot up with me. The gentleman retreated a couple of feet from me.

Miss Sinford noted the movement and said promptly, 'Suffer the little children to come unto me and forbid them not. Child, take this gentleman to your father,' and did her usual vanishing trick into her room next to the front door.

The gentleman regarded me with obvious repulsion, but insisted on helping me up the stairs with the Chariot, which meant that Edward sailed up still sleeping and Avril had a wonderful ride.

Father was at home, reading one of the books from the small battered bookcase which formed part of the furniture of the apartment. He immediately offered his chair to the strange gentleman, who sat down reluctantly as he surveyed the smelly room. His rubicund face, plump figure and well-tailored clothes suggested a successful businessman of some kind.

He cleared his throat, rubbed his well-shaven chin, and said hesitantly, 'I – er – we served in the same regiment – you wrote to our commanding officer. I was asked to call on you.'

Hope lit up my father's face.

The gentleman again cleared his throat, as we stood, tense and silent round him.

'I am authorized to make you a grant of five pounds from our regimental fund, if conditions seem to warrant it.'

He looked round again at the empty fireplace and the ragged, gaunt children watching him breathlessly, and sighed heavily.

Father nodded.

'Could you show me your discharge papers?'

'Yes, indeed I can.'

He took an old business envelope from the top of the bookcase and, from among a pile of birth certificates, finally extracted the precious papers, and handed them to our visitor.

The gentleman examined them.

'You were a private?'

'Yes.'

'I thought you were a lieutenant.'

'I was. I got tired of guarding the East Coast, so I resigned my commission and remustered as a private – and was sent to Russia.'

The gentleman looked very impressed. 'Were you? That was no picnic.'

They went on to discuss the Russian campaign for a few minutes, while the children continued to watch in rapt attention. Alan's hands were clenched together as if in supplication.

Five whole pounds! Would he give it?

He smiled and drew out his wallet, and the sound of a tremendous sigh of relief went through the children. Brian shouted 'Hooray' and went bounding round the room, his little monkey face alight as it had not been for weeks. We all laughed hysterically and escorted our bountiful visitor affectionately down the stairs.

Mother came home and was told the good news and it was wonderful to me to see her expression relax and some of the tenseness go out of her.

Alan and I were immediately despatched to buy a vast quantity of fish and chips and peas and milk, and we spent a blissful ten minutes of anticipation, standing in the steam of the fish-and-chip shop among a shabby, hungry crowd, while the fish sizzled in a great vat of boiling fat.

A fat, sharp-eyed little man, who kept a newspaper and tobacco shop near by, heard me give a big order to the shopkeeper.

'Ain't you the kids from No. 12?' he asked.

'Yes,' replied Alan.

'Got a lot of money to throw around tonight, ain't yer?'

'A man from Daddy's regiment gave us five pounds,' said Alan frankly.

The man's eyes gleamed malevolently.

'Eeee! 'e did, did 'e. Well, yer can tell yer Dad fra' me that I'll be coming over ternight. Yea, ternight!'

The last word came out like a small explosion and was obviously a threat.

Alan whitened visibly, though he answered quite steadily, 'I'll tell Daddy.'

We picked up the two big newspaper parcels handed us by the fish-and-chip merchant, paid for them with a pound note, grabbed our change, and ran down the steps and through the gloomy, gas-lit streets as if pursued by ghosts. We knew instinctively what the newspaper-shop man was. He was a Creditor! Creditors had crowded round Daddy before and caused all our troubles.

'Do you think he'll take our five pounds?' I panted to Alan.

'Not all of it,' said Alan defiantly. 'We'll have finished the fish and chips before he gets to our house. Let's get the milk quickly.'

Not even the colossal row which immediately broke out between my parents when we told them about the Creditor, could dim the pleasure of eating, really eating, once more. My fish and chips and peas were cold by the time I had fed Edward and got the children settled at their meal, but they still tasted like a meal fit for a king.

'Well, where did you think I got the cigarettes from?' asked Father, his teeth deep in fish.

'I never considered the matter,' said Mother haughtily.

I had been so used to seeing my parents smoke, that it had never struck me to question the source of the supply of cigarettes which I had sometimes seen them consume lately.

'How did you imagine you would pay for them?' she inquired.

'I didn't know. I *had* to have a smoke. You smoked them, too!'

Mother began to cry, while Father phlegmatically started to gnaw at another piece of fish.

'I don't know how you persuaded him to trust you,' she sniffed unhappily.

I knew how he had obtained credit. I had already discovered that a good Oxford accent was a much respected asset. A man who spoke as Father did would be trusted by working-class people; they would be sure in their minds that a man who was so well spoken and refined would have the means to pay, no matter how shabby he was.

At that moment there was a knock on the door of the room, and a fearful silence fell upon us all.

Trying not to tremble, I opened the door to reveal an irate member of the working class, our Creditor.

'I want me money,' he said grimly.

'How much?' asked Father, licking his fingers as he got up.

'You know! Thirty-seven and sixpence – and I want it all. Pack o' bloody liars, the lot o' ye,' and he glared around the room.

'Here,' said Father, counting out the money, 'and get out before I throw you out for swearing in front of a lady.'

Quite undaunted, the little man carefully pocketed the money before he moved.

'Lady!' he sneered. 'Ha.'

Father was very neatly made, though by no means tall. His face went red, and he charged straight at the offender, who shot down the first flight of stairs with a nimbleness which would have done credit to a ballet dancer, from which comparatively safe refuge he shook his fist, and then continued downward.

Mother had sat silently through the exchange. Alan and I looked at each other. I could see his visions of plenty to eat for days mixed up with hopes of a new pair of socks slowly fading away. Thirty-seven and sixpence was more than a quarter of the regiment's grant. My own dreams of a broom to sweep with and piles and piles of soap lay shattered.

Fiona, who had not understood anything except the threat of a fight, whimpered and ran to me, and made me take a further step towards growing up.

I put my arms around her and said, with reassuring cheerfulness, 'Daddy still has lots of money left, haven't you, Daddy? We'll be able to have fish and chips again tomorrow, won't we?'

Father had come back into the room and was standing looking worn out in front of the fireplace, but he caught his cue.

'Of course, Fiona, of course we will. Don't worry, little girl. Fish and chips tomorrow.'

Brian suddenly vomited. It seemed to me the worst possible waste of good fish and chips.

CHAPTER FOURTEEN

Mother went to town on a shopping expedition the following morning, while Edward, Avril and I went to the pawnbroker's to redeem my overcoat.

The pawnbroker hailed his blue-eyed duck with pleasure, when, trembling with apprehension at my unaccustomed task, I entered the dark, back part of his shop, pawn-ticket in hand.

He smiled at us both, his dark face gleaming in the poor light like a portrait by Frans Hals.

'Sit the little girl up on the counter, while I deal with these ladies,' he told me cheerfully.

I lifted Avril on to the high counter.

The counter was divided up into three by means of partitions, so as to give people a little privacy in their transactions, and in the next cubicle were a couple of Irish women in black shawls and white aprons. They had each brought their husband's best suit to pawn, since both men had got ships and gone to sea.

The pawnbroker pulled down his waistcoat over his bursting waistline.

'Now, ladies?'

'Himself sailed last night, and a bloody good riddance to him, I say.'

A bundled-up suit was pushed over the counter.

'Will you get an allotment?' asked the pawnbroker, as he inspected the seams of the jacket for wear.

'Och, for sure. Not much though – himself will see to that.'

'I won't be seeing you for a while then, once that starts to come in.'

'And will it be breaking your heart?' She dug a stout elbow into her friend's ribs, and they both chortled.

'I don't think I'll be able to live without you.'

And so on, bickering about how much the suits were worth – worth more than shiftless husbands, I gathered – until finally they swayed out of the shop, their layers of black skirts giving out an unbelievable stench as they moved.

Mother had given me three shillings, which I handed to the pawnbroker with his receipt for the coat. He gave it to his gangling young assistant, who disappeared up a ladder into the loft. A bundle wrapped in a piece of cloth was tossed down and neatly caught by the pawnbroker.

'There you are. When you bring it back, wrap it in the cloth again,' he said kindly. 'Everything has to be wrapped up in a bundle.' He pushed the tightly wrapped package over the counter to me. 'You should undo it and check it.'

I did this and my hopelessly crushed coat was revealed.

'Would threepence buy an iron?' I asked, emboldened by his amiable manner.

His black eyebrows shot up and his sharp brown eyes looked at me shrewdly, when he heard me speak. He rubbed his chin thoughtfully.

'Not from me,' he replied. 'You might get one from the junk-yard at the back.'

He turned, and shouted up the shute to the store-room above, 'George! Mind shop! I'm going out back a minute.'

George came tumbling down the ladder, and I lifted Avril off the counter, where she had been contentedly kicking her heels and watching the proceedings.

We went out through the back door, and through the pawnbroker's yard. The yard was paved with brick, and neat flower-beds filled with daffodils lined the high walls. A hut next to the back gate presumably held a lavatory. He opened the gate and we crossed the narrow alley separating the two lines of business properties, and went into a yard piled high with rusting iron – all the domestic debris of the neighbourhood, from old bedsteads to hip baths.

'Hey, Joe! Where are ye? Got any old flat irons?'

An aged, hunch-backed gnome emerged from under a lean-to. He peered at us from under a greasy, black cap, with the bright perky look of a blackbird. I had often heard him calling through the streets as he pushed his hand-cart along, 'Any rags, bottles or bones? Any old rags today?' His cry would bring the children rushing to him, armed with jamjars or rags to trade for a windmill or some other small toy.

'Humph,' he grunted. 'Ah might 'ave.'

He rooted through a collection of old kitchen pails, washboards and dollies lying under an ancient wooden mangle, and finally came up with a small, rusty iron, which he agreed to part with for threepence.

Back in the pawnbroker's shop, I was made to wait while George was instructed to find a piece of sandpaper and rub the iron clean for me.

Gold teeth flashing amid tobacco-stained white ones, the pawnbroker finally presented me with quite a respectable-looking iron.

'There ye are, luv,' he said.

'Thank you very, very much,' I said, and swept out, iron in hand, my coat with its attendant bit of cloth over my arm, and a protesting Avril held firmly by the other hand.

'I want to stay here,' she yelled. 'I like it here.'

I had not forgotten the awful scarecrow I had seen in the Bold Street shop window, however, and I took Edward and her straight home, because I was determined to make a fire with some of the coal the regimental grant had enabled us to buy, heat water and wash myself.

This I did, though I had no soap. I hoped Mother would buy plenty of washing soap, so that I could wash my clothes too. I knew that our family looked far more neglected than many children did.

I had pressed my coat reasonably well by the time Mother came home. She was laden with socks, vests, a real towel, a wash bowl, some cups, saucers and plates, knives and forks, a saucepan, some Aspirin, some cigarettes, and, best of all, some toilet soap and soap powder.

It was Friday, and, when the children came home, I stripped their clothes off them, put on their overcoats, which they considered a great joke, and washed everything. Soon the room was festooned with steaming garments.

Then I washed the children thoroughly, one by one. They were all emaciated, bug-bitten and shaky on their feet in spite of their two fish-and-chip dinners. Only years later, when I saw pictures of the prisoners released from Belsen, did I fully realize how close we were to dying of starvation, and also what an ordeal it must have been for those children at school to drag themselves there and back and try to pay attention while their bodies gradually wasted.

Nobody in the school seemed to notice the children's suffering. The school nurse found that their hair was verminous, and sent a note to say that we should buy a certain kind of ointment and rub it into their scalps. We had no money for ointment, however, so nothing was done.

No priest of any denomination ever came to see us, though the school was a Church school and a Church of England minister came once or twice to visit Miss Sinford. We knew that we were too dirty and shabby to be welcome in a church, and, except for any religious instruction the children might have received in school, God, like Santa Claus, went out of our lives.

For some time, our only entertainment was to walk the streets and look in shop windows, but gradually the younger ones found ways of amusing themselves. Better weather brought little urchins out to play cricket, with a piece of wood for a bat and a couple of beer bottles for wickets, and my brothers were tolerated in these games. Fiona and Avril learned from Fiona's schoolfriends how to skip and play hopscotch on the pavement in front of the house. They all quickly learned to scream and swear with an unlovely Liverpool accent, though they did not do so in their own home.

I read all the books in the small bookcase in our room. I often read while washing the dishes or feeding the baby and it was then that I discovered that a book laid on the cover of the Chariot could be read while pushing it along the street. I waded through a curious collection of reading matter, including *Hadji Baba of Isphahan, Ideal Marriage,* most of Walter Scott's works, a handbook for midwives and several copies of *Moore's Almanac.*

With the last few pennies from the grant from the regiment, Father enrolled himself and Mother in the local branch of the public library, and immediately life seemed filled with untold riches, because I, too, could obtain books on their tickets. The modest little building had a certain elegance – and it was warm. I could not sit in it for hours, as Father did, because I had Edward and Avril always with me and they could not keep quiet for long, but I eagerly snatched books from the shelves and read avidly and haphazardly.

In her shopping list, Mother had included a packet of needles and darning wool and black and white cotton. I now spent most of my evenings darning socks, since nylon socks were not yet on the market, and doing other mending, until the cotton and wool ran out.

The good effect of the regimental grant remained with us, in some degree, for several weeks, though we were still verminous, still had no change of clothing, and were desperate over the need for shoe repairs and, indeed, for new shoes, particularly in the spring rain. We searched the second-hand shops for old running-shoes, anything to cover our feet. Even a few pence spent on such things, however, meant that we could not, at times, have even enough starches to eat. Mother and I found it ever more difficult to drag ourselves up and down the endless stairs; and Father looked like a scarecrow.

Would it ever end, I wondered; and then was

seized with childish terror that it might end in death.

Then, in April Mother got a job. She had tried recently for domestic work, but well-to-do housewives did not want a refined woman to scrub their floors; it made them feel uncomfortable. She had also tried all the city shops. But many of them employed, as far as possible, girls under sixteen years of age, and dismissed them on their sixteenth birthday, because at that age they had to pay to the government heavier National Health and unemployment insurance contributions for them. The number of women seeking work was so great that some stores demanded and got girls of matriculation standard to run their lifts and clean their lavatories. Almost all of those who survived their sixteenth birthday in employment, lost their jobs when they were eighteen because at that age, again, the employers' contributions to their insurance went up. Perhaps it was as well that my parents did not know that in Liverpool unemployment was rapidly reaching a peak of 31.5 per cent, one of the highest in the country; they were close enough to suicide as it was.

Mother's employer was a slippery eel of a man who lived near-by. In his kitchen, he mixed that old-fashioned spring remedy, brimstone and treacle, filled ice-cream cartons with it, and sold it door-to-door for threepence and sixpence a pot, according to size. He had done so well that he decided to employ Mother on a commission basis. She would receive a halfpenny on a small pot and a penny on any larger pot she sold.

Unaware of the need for a pedlar's licence, Mother set out hopefully to knock on the front doors of the better class districts, her supply of brimstone and treacle carried in a paper bag.

Since she had a very dignified presence, not many doors were slammed in her face, and at the end of a six-day week she found she had made seven shillings and sixpence and her tram fares. The weather had mercifully been fine and the steady walking had strengthened her muscles. Moreover, a number of kindly housewives had helped her along with cups of tea and biscuits.

It was agreed that her wages must be spent on new shoes for her, so that she could continue to work. I tucked my bare feet under the rickety table. Mother looked really animated for the first time since we had arrived in Liverpool, and took a penny tram-ride to town at our urging, to buy the precious shoes.

Mother's modest success at her first job dimmed

considerably any hope I had of ever being able to go to school again; it was as if a jailer had clanged shut yet another prison door between me and freedom. I realized abruptly how deeply I had hoped she would prove a failure at work, so that she would be forced to stay at home and take over from me her normal duties as a mother. I felt wretched and could comfort myself only with the thought that when Father got work I might stand a chance of going to school, since possibly Mother would then feel there was no necessity for her to work.

After she had left for town, I bumped the Chariot slowly down the stairs. Edward who, by now, was trying to sit up, hit his head when I went over a stair more clumsily than usual and started to cry. Avril, who was hungry and tired, joined in.

At the bottom of the stairs, an infuriated Mr Ferris awaited me. His droopy yellow moustache was fluffed out as he blew through it with rage and his eyes bulged like a Pekinese dog's.

'What the hell are you doing, making such a noise?' he shouted.

I stared blankly at him, not knowing how to reply.

'I can't practise with such a racket. I won't stand

for it! You'll have to go. Mrs Foster will have to put you out!'

Miss Sinford came through her door, like the old lady on a weather vane.

'Thou shalt not take the Name of the Lord in vain,' she said primly to Mr Ferris. 'I am preparing to go to Communion. Kindly be quiet.'

'I have not taken Him in vain,' roared Mr Ferris, his false teeth threatening to come out, as he nearly spat at her.

Miss Sinford shook a blue-veined fist at him.

'Go back to your piano, sir,' she squeaked. 'And pray for forgiveness for your bad temper.'

I stood between them as they ranted at each other, so filled with fear that I could not move.

He had said: 'You'll have to go! Mrs Foster will have to put you out!'

'Oh no, O Lord,' I prayed. 'Nobody else will ever take us in. We'll have to go to the workhouse. Don't, please don't, let Mrs Foster turn us out.'

Miss Sinford had dived past the Chariot and struck Mr Ferris a sharp blow on the nose, and, like a terrified rabbit, I was suddenly galvanized into trying to escape.

Hastily, I manoeuvred the Chariot past the contestants, through the front door and down the worn steps to the street. Fear beat at me, and

I ran as fast as the Chariot and its two wailing passengers would allow me to.

I ran blindly through the grey streets and did not stop until my stick-like legs began to fail me and I found myself on Princes Avenue.

The workhouse or Institution, as it had recently been renamed, loomed like a scarifying black shadow over all the destitute of England; even I knew that. And I was ready to die of fear.

CHAPTER FIFTEEN

Very slowly, I trundled the Chariot down the Avenue. The trees which lined it were in leaf, and each leaf of the privet hedges in the small town gardens in front of the houses looked as if it had been specially polished. On the stone-flagged pavement the puddles from recent rain were drying up under a mild sun. It was mid-afternoon and very quiet. My teeth gradually stopped chattering, and Avril ceased her lament and demanded to be lifted out so that she could walk.

When I picked her up out of the pram she felt remarkably light, even in my wasted arms, and my teeth again began to chatter like castanets, as I looked down at her. She began to toddle along contentedly, however, singing in a rasping little voice 'Little Bo Peep' which we had been practising together.

The warmth of the sun and the peace had its effect. Perhaps, I argued to myself, 'Mr Parish' or even Daddy's regiment would protect us from the ire of Mr Ferris. I stopped in the middle of the pavement and smiled to myself, as I visualized Father's regiment marching down the street, their putteed legs moving in purposeful unison, to rescue us from Mr Ferris.

'Frog's eyes! Frog's eyes!' shouted a rough voice in my ear, and a couple of big boys made playful snatches at my spectacles.

Avril screamed. I instinctively clutched at the precious spectacles. They laughed, and quickly kicked my shins with their heavy boots. Screaming wildly, they ran on down the Avenue, leaving me quivering with pain and mortification.

'Beasts!' shouted Avril after them, with considerable spirit.

Crying quietly with pain, I walked on into Princes Park and into the rose garden which, though as yet bare of roses, was a pretty place, with a little lake much favoured by ducks and other small water birds.

My legs felt like jelly and I thought I was going to faint, so I sat down on the first bench we could find. At the other end of the seat was an old gentleman. He was shabbily, though respectably, dressed, with a stiff winged collar encircling a thin, turtle-like neck. A heavily moustached, sallow face was framed by a trilby hat set a little to the back of his head. His expression was benign and he had an air of quiet dignity. He was persuing a small, leatherbound book.

Avril came to sit on my knee, and I began to teach her the names of the various kinds of ducks swimming on the lake. The faintness receded and I forgot my bruised shins.

Our peace was soon broken.

'Hey, you there with the pram! Get out o' here! No children allowed in this here garden without an adult.' A uniformed park attendant was waving a stick at us from the rose-garden gate.

Because I did not immediately respond – I was still unaccustomed to my reduction to the ranks of the under-privileged – he started down the path towards us, his stick raised menacingly.

Without warning, a quiet commanding voice beside me said, 'The children are with me. I am responsible for them.'

The old gentleman had closed his book, and was staring coldly at the attendant.

The parkkeeper lowered his stick and looked disbelievingly at the old gentleman, who gazed back calmly at him, until finally the parkkeeper, his lips curled in a sneer, grunted, 'Humph!' and turned away, to continue his promenade through the park.

In a quiet voice, with an accent that might have been French, the old gentleman asked me, 'And where did you learn to speak English like that, child?'

I blushed guiltily. He must have been listening to Avril and me.

What was wrong with my English? And how does one learn one's own language? I asked myself. I was nonplussed.

Sharp brown eyes, with yellowed whites, appraised my bare feet, greasy gym slip, worn without a blouse, which I had had to lend to Fiona, and knitted cardigan with holes through which my elbows stuck.

Ashamed, I bowed my head so that my face was shielded by a mass of untended hair.

'I . . . er . . . I learned it at home,' I muttered.

'You speak it beautifully,' he said with a gentle smile. 'I have not heard better speech during my many years in Liverpool.' The intonation was definitely foreign.

The bent head shot up. This was the first compliment anyone had ever paid me.

'Do you really think so?' I asked incredulously.

'I do.'

I said impulsively, 'Mummy and Nanny thought it was important to speak well. Neither of them seemed to think that I spoke very well.'

'Nanny?'

I nodded confusedly.

'We don't have a nurse now.'

A watery sniff muffled the much admired accent.

He said dryly, 'I imagine not.'

Avril clambered down off my knee and went on one of her small perambulations. Edward slept. My acquaintance opened his book, as if to continue his reading. Instead, he sat tapping the page with a swollen, chilblained finger.

My eyes were carried to the page by the pointing finger, and I was astonished to see that the print in the book consisted of curly dashes with occasional dots.

He noticed my interest, and smiled at me.

'It is Arabic,' he said.

I was impressed.

'Can you speak it, sir?'

'Of course. My mother was an Arab.'

That accounted for the darker skin, I thought, and I wondered if I dare ask him what brought him to England. How romantic to have a real Arab for a mother! I wondered if she wore a yashmak and transparent trousers, like the princesses in my fairy-tale books.

His eyes were twinkling. Perhaps he was lonely, too, for he said suddenly, 'I speak seven languages and can read four more.'

'How wonderful!' I exclaimed in genuine admiration, remembering my own struggles with the French language.

'Tell me,' he said. 'How is it that – that—' and he waved his hand in a comprehensive gesture, which took in the Chariot with its half-starved baby and Avril's and my deplorable condition.

Hesitating and seeking for words at first, I explained as best I could about bankruptcy and unemployment. Gradually I gained courage and confided in him my despair at not being able to continue at school and my fear of what would become of us.

He listened patiently, occasionally interjecting a question or nodding understandingly.

Finally I trailed to a hopeless stop.

He sat silent for a while, contemplating the lake, his book still open on his knee, his face full of the sad resignation of the very old.

At last, he sighed and said, 'You know, child, it is not what happens to you that matters – it is how you deal with it.'

This was a new idea to me and I pondered on it, as I shyly watched his face.

'You can read?'

'Yes.'

'You go to the library?'

'Yes.'

'Then read! Read everything you can. Read the great historians, the philosophers, especially the German ones, read autobiographies, read novels. One day, you will have the opportunity to make use of the knowledge you will accumulate, and you will be surprised to find that you know much more than those who have had a more formal education.'

He closed his book and put it in his pocket, and then said quite cheerfully, 'Your day will come, child. Your parents are having a difficult time at present and cannot help you.'

He got up from his seat slowly and stiffly and then bowed politely to me.

'I come here every sunny afternoon to commune with nature. Come one day and tell me what you have read.'

The faintness which had threatened me before was making his face dim to me, but I thanked him warmly and promised that I would come. I felt wonderfully comforted.

I sat down again after he had left, to allow my faintness to recede. Then I called Avril and hastened out of the rose garden before the keeper could find us without a guardian.

The way home seemed infinitely long and the momentary peace engendered by the conversation with the old man gradually left me, to be replaced with memories of Dickens's descriptions of workhouses.

CHAPTER SIXTEEN

When I arrived home, Alan and Fiona were sitting on the bottom step of the imposing flight of steps which led up to the front door of Mrs Foster's house. The evening was drawing on and the lamplighter was going on his rounds, pulling on the gas lights with his long rod as he paused, wobbling on his bicycle, at each lamp-post.

Alan was talking cheerfully to Fiona, who looked white and woebegone, her blue eyes wide and her china-doll features crumpled with fear.

'What's the matter?' I asked in some alarm, as I stopped the Chariot beside them.

Alan peered up at me through his tousled mop of yellow hair.

'Fiona's scared, and I'm telling her that there is nothing to be scared about,' he said stoutly.

Trying not to show that I was frightened, I lifted Avril out of the Chariot with elaborate casualness and clucked encouragingly at Edward, who smiled at me angelically.

I sat down beside Alan.

'What *is* the matter?'

Fiona answered through trembling lips.

'Mrs Foster is shouting at Mother, and Mother is shouting at Father – and – and it's an awful noise.

'And I want to go home to Nanny!' And she began to cry.

'Be quiet!' I snapped at her, and she was immediately reduced to cowed silence.

I turned to Alan.

'Has Mr Ferris complained?'

Alan looked puzzled.

'Mr Ferris? You mean about the noise we make?'

'Yes.'

'Oh no.' Alan chuckled suddenly and began to play an imaginary piano with gusto. 'He makes too much noise himself. He just shouts at us because it makes him feel better.' He tossed back his hair, exactly as Mr Ferris did, and finished his piano piece with a mighty boom on the bottom notes, 'Boom-tiddly-boom – boo-om – boom!'

I wished that I had Alan's cool common sense.

In one sentence he had calmed my fears. But not Fiona's apparently. Tears were running down her cheeks like raindrops.

'What has happened, then?'

Alan sobered.

'Daddy didn't pay the rent. He spent the money on cigarettes, and Mrs Foster is as cross as two sticks. And Mother is crossest of all, because she helped to smoke the cigarettes without thinking of where they came from. And – well, you know Mother.'

I did know Mother. Even in her most halcyon days, her temper had been something to avoid at all costs. Now, sick, bewildered, hungry and despairing, her bouts of temper bordered on insanity. She was terrifying in her rages, more terrifying in her subsequent withdrawn silences.

I licked my lips and voiced my dread in a whisper, so as not to frighten Avril, who was sitting on the pavement playing with two matchsticks and a piece of orange-peel. Alan and Fiona bent their heads close to mine.

'Do you think she'll turn us out into the street – Mrs Foster, I mean?'

'No idea,' replied Alan phlegmatically. 'Fiona and I just opened the door when we came back from school, and understood what the trouble was inside a minute. So we just left them to it – and came down here.'

'Where are Brian and Tony?'

Alan sighed. 'They bounced right into the room. Now they'll be expected to take sides – and Brian will have nightmares – and probably be sick after tea.'

I nodded silent agreement. Poor Brian, sensitive to every nuance of every word spoken to him, would be reduced to incoherence by such an episode.

'Have we got bread for tea?' asked Fiona.

'A little,' I said.

'Shall we ever have butter again?'

'Of course,' said Alan.

Avril toddled up to us.

'I like jam as well as butter,' she announced. 'I want jam for tea.'

I suppressed an irrational desire to slap Avril, and we sat quietly watching seamen crowding into the hall of a house opposite to ours. In this house lived an assortment of middle-aged women, who were a great mystery to me. They were much better dressed than their neighbours, though they never seemed to go out to work. And they had lots of visitors – all men.

I watched the rolling gait of the men lounging

up the steps. Many of them were already drunk. They shouted raucously to each other and laughed at remarks of which I did not get the import.

One of the single ladies who lived on the same floor as Mrs Foster, came down our steps and paused by us. She looked across the road and then regarded us uneasily.

'Dawn't yer think ye'd better go in, luv?' she asked.

I looked up at her dully. She seemed magnificent to me with her veiled, flowered hat and flashing diamanté earrings. Her silver evening shoes and rayon stockings were close to me, however, and she did not smell very nice.

Uneasily, I turned my head away.

'We can't,' I said.

'Daddy and Mummy are cross,' announced Avril, rising from the pavement and dusting down her little backside.

The lady bit her scarlet lower lip, as she considered this, and then said in confidential tones to me, 'Eee, luv, ah think you had better get inside. Over there is going to be ruddy noisy – and rough to the likes o' you. There's four ships in.'

Though none of us knew what she meant, we rose reluctantly and Alan helped me pull the Chariot up the steps.

I appreciated that she had tried to be kind to us, and I thanked her, as she started to walk with swaying hips to the bus stop at the corner.

'That's all right, luv,' she said cheerfully, and she hitched her mangy fox fur up round her chin and called to Avril, 'Now, run along, luv.'

'She's pretty kind, isn't she?' I remarked to Alan, as we jointly heaved the Chariot up the stairs to the top of the house, from whence the sounds of battle still proceeded.

'Yes,' said Alan. But he did not sound convinced, though he added, 'She gave me a sweet the other day.'

Just as we were about to tackle the last flight of stairs, we heard Mrs Foster's heavy tread coming down. We cringed together on the landing as, without a word, she passed us, her black georgette draperies floating around her. Behind her she left a mixed odour of cats and birds.

Dead silence greeted us as we entered our room. My parents occupied the two kitchen chairs which the room boasted. Their mouths were clamped shut, and only my mother's fast breathing told of the earlier strife. Brian was biting his nails feverishly, as he stood watching them. Tony was calmly playing with a pebble on the table, pretending it was a train: he muttered 'chuff-chuff-chuff' to himself as he ran it into a station. He looked up as we entered, his large intelligent eyes sad with a sadness unnatural in one so young.

'Hello, Helen,' he said, his voice sounding loud in the prevailing quietness. 'What about some tea – it's late.'

I did not know what to do about my parents, so I ignored them and answered him.

'Yes, dear. Just let me unload.'

From around Edward's feet in the pram, I exhumed a mass of small pieces of rubbish, which I had gleaned during my walk, and laid them in the hearth. There were empty match-boxes, cigarette cartons – which did not usually burn very well – bits of stick, twigs and paper of every description, and a whole tattered copy of the *Liverpool Echo*.

I raked through the cold ashes in the grate and salvaged a few cinders. Would I have enough fuel to boil some water, I wondered anxiously.

Alan kindly volunteered to run down to the bathroom and fetch a pan of water, and Fiona, without being asked, took Edward on her knee. She gasped as his wet napkin damped her gym slip and bare legs, but she did not complain. And all the time my parents sat in silence, almost prostrated by their quarrels.

It was nearly dark by the time the water was

persuaded to boil and the tea was made. I cut a dry, white loaf into eight pieces of roughly equal size, and gave each of my parents a piece of it with a cup of the smoky tea, which had, of course, no milk or sugar in it. I gave a little tea to each child in whatever receptacles I could muster, with a piece of bread.

'Can I dip?' asked Tony. 'The crust is too hard to bite.'

I looked at my mother, who ignored the question and stared moodily into her teacup.

My father picked up his cup, and said suddenly, 'You may.'

Thankfully, Tony and Brian plunged their bread into their tea.

'The bread is so stale it's second-hand,' remarked Tony.

Brian giggled and snorted helplessly into his jam-jar of tea. 'I've got a second-hand teacup to match,' he gurgled, a note of hysteria in his voice.

'I want some jam,' shouted Avril.

'Be quiet, Avril,' said Fiona, who had given a little of her bread to Edward to suck on. 'You know there is no jam.'

'Not even any second-hand jam?' the younger girl demanded with mock indignation.

My father began to laugh, at first a small wry chuckle in his throat and, then, gaining momentum, one of his old hearty laughs. I joined in, and soon the whole family was laughing hysterically, the noise pealing along the cobwebbed ceiling and down the stairs to the floor below, where the other tenants, hearing us, must have believed us to be mad.

Only Mother, wrapped in pain, fatigue and semi-starvation, sat silently staring at her cup of tea, her piece of bread in her hand.

CHAPTER SEVENTEEN

We crept through the spring and summer, cursing wet days, rejoicing in warm, dry ones, ignoring petty ailments and hunger, since we could do nothing about either.

Several of the children had sores which took a long time to heal. These were sometimes caused by normal cuts and abrasions, acquired while playing, going septic; and sometimes from their scratching at their vermin-ridden bodies. We nearly all suffered from toothache from time to time, and Mother's teeth began to loosen. Brian suffered torture from gumboils. His first teeth had been good but he had several large cavities in his second ones, caused, perhaps, by the large amount of white bread in his diet. His wizened face would swell up and he would cry hour after hour, until finally the abscess would burst and the pain would be reduced. On one occasion his weeping was heard as far away as the basement of the house; and Mrs Hicks, prodded by her out-of-work, bricklayer husband, made the long journey up the stairs, to inquire what was the matter.

'He's got a bad tooth,' I explained. 'He can't go to school today, because it hurts too much.'

'Well, poor luv!' she exclaimed, her double chin, with its little crown of spiky hairs, wobbling sympathetically. 'Na, then, I got some oil of cloves. Come daanstairs with me, luv,' she called to Brian, who was hovering nervously in the background. 'Ah got somethin' as will help yer. Come on, na.'

Brian allowed himself to be beguiled downstairs, where he spent the afternoon lying on Mrs Hicks's horsehair sofa in front of her blazing fire, having hot cloths put on his cheeks and quantities of bitter oil of cloves dabbed into his cavities.

Nobody had ever made such a fuss of him, and, despite the pain and the foul taste of oil of cloves, he loved it. He loved also the warmth, the cosiness and the old tin teapot keeping its contents warm on the hob.

Mr Hicks called him a brave lad, and, when he was feeling better, and was ready to return to our cold, clammy apartment, Mrs Hicks invited him to come down again on a day when his teeth were not hurting, and have a cup of tea and a homemade scone with them.

He came back full of glee, in spite of his swollen face, and remained Mr and Mrs Hicks's devoted friend and message-runner for years.

The Hickses had so little, and yet they managed to make their dark basement so cosy. Mrs Hicks must have been an excellent housekeeper and, unlike many of her neighbours, she understood the nutritional value of many cheap foods like herrings and lentils, and she pointed out to me that brown bread was better than white. My mother, like many middle-class English people at that time, knew very little about the need for a well-balanced diet.

Another good cook was the Spanish lady who had given us the Chariot. I found she had a Spanish husband, who was a warehouseman in one of the fruit warehouses near the Fruit Exchange, and he kept her well supplied with oranges, apples and other delicacies in season. He was, she confided to me as we sat on the steps in the sun, a man of choleric temper and colossal jealousy. But, ah me, what a man!

I smiled sympathetically, and bounced Edward up and down on my knee, to his great delight.

She pulled her black, knitted shawl tightly round her shoulders, and looked at me coquettishly.

'You not understand yet, I think. But you learn.'

'I expect so,' I replied guardedly, not at all sure what I would learn but sensing it would be something interesting.

She cooed in Spanish to Edward.

He could crawl a little now, but he was not a pretty baby. His head, which looked too big, was covered with scurf, and his stomach stuck out grotesquely. His smile, however, was sweet as he responded to the Spanish words.

'My last boy, Peter, he go to school with your Tony. Say your Tony very clever – can read well and do his arithmetic.'

This was news to me, there being no contact between home and school. My father, eternally busy at being unemployed, had given no consideration to his children's progress. My mother, after the brimstone and treacle season came to an end, about the end of May, kept trying unsuccessfully for other work, and long walks to see prospective employers took up much of her time. She was now well, in the sense that she had recovered from Edward's birth and her subsequent major operation, but she was nearly starving and was still walking the razor's edge between mental health and nervous breakdown. She was a mere wreckage of the lovely woman she had been a short eighteen months previously.

The Spanish lady was speaking again.

'What your Dadda work at?'

'He is registered as a bookkeeper-clerk.'

I felt reticent. I did not want to tell our story to anyone who asked, and I parried all further questions.

Frequently, I walked down the avenue to Princes Park and, seated on the sun-warmed bench in the rose garden, had long conversations with the old gentleman who had defended us against the parkkeeper.

'I was never rich,' he once volunteered in his precise English. 'I have always worked as an interpreter – and I still do sometimes interpret for Arab and Chinese seamen in the magistrate's court.'

'Were you born in China, sir?' I ventured.

'No. I was born in Lebanon. My father was a German and, as I think I told you once, Mother was an Arab. So I had three languages – German, Arabic and French, which is widely spoken in Lebanon. Father was an engineer by profession and I had the chance to learn Chinese and English while he was working in Singapore, then Spanish in Mexico and Portuguese in Brazil. I taught myself

Italian.' He paused for breath, and then went on, 'Now I study Greek and Hebrew, so that I can study the Scriptures in more detail.'

I was awed by such a catalogue of learning.

'You must have been able to live quite comfortably,' I hazarded.

'I had sufficient. But, you must know, child, that scholarship does not often bring one money – one can earn, yes – but it is the enrichment of the mind rather than of the pocket which it gives.' He laughed softly. 'I was rich in friends, a good wife, three sons . . .' His voice broke, and he stopped.

'Do your boys live with you?' I inquired, wondering that he had not mentioned them before.

He looked at me absently.

'My boys – my wonderful boys – all died in the war. My dear wife followed them three years ago. Soon I shall join them.' He snapped his little book shut as if to show how suddenly he would finish.

I was ashamed at having pried into his affairs. Adult suffering had a way of springing upon one from unexpected sources, and I had yet to learn how heavy a burden the adult world carried at times.

'I'm truly sorry to have been so impertinent,' I mumbled.

I hoped passionately that he would not die. He

was the only clean, civilized person I knew in Liverpool; and he was as wise as my grandmother, who lived so far away, a whole twopence away, in the Wirral. That my parents were civilized did not occur to me. They always seemed to be so far away from me.

The old gentleman shook his depression away, realized I was distressed and comforted me.

'When you are eighty-one years old, you look forward to being once more with your loved ones,' he said.

We sat quietly together. I tended to agree with him that death was something to look forward to.

'Do you believe in God – and Heaven?' I asked timidly.

'Yes, indeed,' he said. 'My mother was a Mohammedan and my father was a Lutheran, and neither impressed a religion upon me. They both explained their beliefs to me, but they made me study and search for God.'

'We are Church of England,' I said. 'That is . . .' I hesitated. 'That is, when we are clean and rich we are Church of England. I suppose at present we are nothing.' I laughed a little guiltily. 'I have never been inside a church in Liverpool. When we were at home, the minister called from time to time

– but he does not do so here. I suppose we are too wicked.'

He sat contemplating the placid lake for a minute, and then asked, 'Has nobody from your Church been to see you?'

'Yes. When we first came, a very kind priest in a long black robe brought us some food. He was very nice. I do not think our present house is in his parish.'

'You should go to your parish church.'

'We could not,' I replied emphatically. 'We are so dirty – we can't afford soap.'

He nodded understandingly.

I added, 'I do not know what we did to deserve it all.'

He smiled gently.

'God tries us all, child. Pray to Him for help. He will hear you.'

I thanked him, and got up heavily from the bench. There was no hope in me.

All the way home, however, I prayed silently in the well-known words of the Anglican prayer-book, in the belief that there is no harm in trying.

CHAPTER EIGHTEEN

One of the penalties frequently paid for being poor is that of being cut off from the rest of the world. The normal means of communication such as newspapers, radio and letters cost money. Some of our neighbours had radios, and they clung to them no matter what else they had to part with. It was their main source of both entertainment and news, as long as they had a penny to put into the electric meter or could afford to get the wet batteries recharged. These families could hear the first rumbling of the Nazi movement in Germany and Mussolini's fiery speeches, and of strikes and riots in Spain, the prelude to the Spanish Civil War. Nearer home, there was the crisis of the resignation of the Labour Government.

My father read several national newspapers and

the *Liverpool Echo* whenever he went to the library. My mother, also, would skim through the *Echo* during a quick visit to the library, when she would jot down on a piece of paper details of jobs advertised. They were, however, the exception; most people around us found reading a laborious effort and there was a fair sprinkling among the older inhabitants who could neither read nor write.

The newspaper room in the library seemed to be the preserve of adults, who did not like a dirty ragamuffin with a baby on her hip, pushing in front of them. In consequence, I knew more about Walsingham and Lord Burghley, Queen Elizabeth I's ministers, than I did about George V's Ramsay MacDonald.

I knew nobody of my own age and was cut off from all forms of play. Some girls of about fourteen years of age lived in the vicinity. They were tough, brassy lasses, who regarded themselves as adults and worked all day in factories or shops. Each girl had a best friend who was known as her mate and together they went to the cinema or to dances, where they danced together; if a boy asked one of them for a dance she circled the floor with him in silence, her face exhibiting about as much expression as the back of a tram. Every Friday evening they solemnly washed and set each other's hair, and on Sundays, dressed in their best, they would walk together in the streets, regarding hopeful males with joint disdain. This was a matriarchal society where ferocious grandmothers and nagging mothers reigned supreme and men seemed to have hardly a toehold in the home, and these young girls were already aware of this.

They were cheap labour and at the age of sixteen they would often be unemployed, like their elder sisters, but in the meantime they were frequently the most affluent members of their household, with money to spend in Woolworth's on cosmetics and rhinestone jewellery. I envied them their neat, black, work dresses and, even more, their best Sunday coats and hats and high-heeled shoes. They never spoke to me, except sometimes to jeer at my rags. At such times my glasses would mist over with tears, and I would whisk Avril and the Chariot round a corner, before the children could realize what was happening.

The local boys bullied both Avril and me, just as they did a subnormal boy who lived in the next street and a little Negress, the daughter of a medical student, who lived round the corner. None of us was human by the standards of these lads – we looked different – and we ranked with dogs and cats, to be teased and mishandled if caught.

Our family received no letters. It was as if everybody we had known before that first day in Liverpool had dropped dead. My parents always hoped for letters in reply to the endless applications for work which they wrote, but nothing arrived. Occasionally, my mother would write to an old acquaintance to beg for financial help in our predicament; there was no response.

I longed passionately to go to school, to have some small communion with a more ordered world where I might find some spark of hope of a better life through learning. I continued to pray that, since my brothers and sisters attended a Church school, the priest would one day call upon us and would discover my existence; I was sure he could make my parents send me to his school. But the Church knew us not, and I was thrown back upon my library books and what I could remember from the past.

Unlike many children, I had always enjoyed going to church. The major festivals of the year were to me wonderful theatrical productions, and my introduction to the works of many great composers had been through hearing their music pouring forth from a well-played organ on such occasions. Some of the churches I had attended were hundreds of years old and had priceless paintings, tapestries, vestments, carvings in stone and wood, magnificent brasswork and gold ornaments, a wealth of beauty on which the myopic eyes of a small girl could feast when the sermon became boring.

The beauty of the language of King James's Version of the Bible and of the Church of England Prayer-Book and the rich poetry of the hymn-book were not lost upon me, and enriched my knowledge of the English tongue.

Now, when mental stimulus was most required and religious comfort desperately needed, these things were gone from us. I believed that God was not just angry with us – he was simply furious.

Apart from being exposed to the scholarship and intellectual wealth of the Church of England, I was fortunate in having well-educated parents. They were extremely modern in their day and surrounded themselves with friends who discussed at length ideas and concepts of the times as well as more mundane matters.

As the eldest child, I was sometimes allowed to leave the nursery and sit with my elders in the drawing-room. Bearing in mind the hissed instructions of Nanny to 'hold my hush', I would sit, like a sleepy owl, on a stool by the white marble fireplace, admiring Mother's collection of Georgian silver which winked at me in the firelight from an antique sideboard.

The drawing-room always seemed to be full of well-tailored gentlemen, some of them economists and bankers, others wealthy merchants; and a younger group clustered round my mother talking witty nonsense to her. I did not always understand what was discussed – I was too young. I soon became aware of the world and its problems, however, as seen through the eyes of the upper middle class. There was a place called the Stock Market inhabited by bulls and bears; and there were far-away countries, like India and China, where men made fortunes. There were terrifying food shortages called famines when men died in the streets; there were wonderful farms, full of sheep, in Australia, and others equally full of wheat in Canada. There were ships to be built, railways to sell and venturesome investments to be made in car, radio and electric-light-bulb firms.

The world was a wonderful, exciting place, and I longed to grow up and be part of it.

Nobody mentioned the kind of world in which I now lived. Perhaps my father's friends did not know of its existence, or, if they did, preferred to forget it. And where were my father's friends?

I kneeled on the floor by the window of our top-floor eyrie and looked down at the unemployed men playing one of their endless games of ollies, a form of marbles. I remembered how Joan had ignored me when I had met her. I supposed that Father's friends had done the same.

So much for friendship.

One form of communication which was very rare in such streets as I looked down upon was telephoning. The public telephone was beginning to make its appearance; but even that assumed that the public had friends or businesses with telephones, to whom they wished to speak. In my new world, families still sent one of the family with either a written or verbal message.

Father had always been interested in French history, particularly the reign of Louis XIV, and I had been with him on a number of interesting trips to museums to see new acquisitions of jewellery, clothing or furniture of this period. It occurred to me, one day, that Avril and I could go to the museum together, so I pushed the little girl and Edward in the Chariot all the way to the city and then across it to William Brown Street. I pulled the Chariot up and down three huge flights of steps until I found the right building, and was just struggling to get the pram through a recalcitrant door when a voice boomed, 'Where are you going with that thing?'

A very large commissionaire stood behind me.

'I'm going to the museum,' I replied nervously.

'Not with that you're not.'

His remark was clear enough, but there was a hint of puzzlement in the tone of his voice when he made it.

I looked sadly down at Avril. I was afraid to leave the Chariot outside, in case some urchin thought it was abandoned and took it to play with.

I looked up at the commissionaire and was prepared to do battle.

He must have seen the malignant gleam in my eye, because he said sharply, 'Now you just take that thing back to where you found it, and don't let me find you loitering round here again.'

Loitering was something one could be arrested for, I knew, so I swallowed the bitter words that came to mind, and silently turned and bounced the Chariot back down the steps so fast that I cannonaded into an elderly, distinguished-looking gentleman coming up.

'Oh, I beg your pardon, sir,' I said, horrified at having struck such a gentle, scholarly type of person. 'I hope I haven't hurt you badly.'

'Not at all. My briefcase took the blow,' he

replied kindly, as he stared in surprise at Avril and me. His lips parted, as if to ask me something, but I had been so humiliated by the commissionaire that I felt I was going to cry, and I hastened onward across the street to St George's Hall. Once there, I looked back.

The gentleman was standing at the door of the museum still staring curiously at me.

I giggled suddenly through my tears. An Oxford accent coming from a bundle of rags and bones like me must have really puzzled him. It had not, however, impressed the commissionaire and gained me entry to the museum.

So much for public cultural emporia.

CHAPTER NINETEEN

Summertime had always meant to me a period of waving green wheat slowly turning yellow, a time for walks along a meadow-bordered river where buttercups waited to be threaded into chains, a time to lie under a plum-tree and read to my heart's content, a time to play at theatres and dressing-up with my friend, Joan, while the walnuts ripened overhead.

Liverpool summers are not like that. In the nineteen-thirties not much was understood about pollution; and on days when it did not rain the acrid smoke was enough to obscure the sun until a harsh, Atlantic wind temporarily lifted the veil. On hot days the alleyways and garbage cans stank, despite the ministrations of an army of dustmen who not only laboriously cleared the garbage but also washed down the alleys themselves. There were still a lot of horses in Liverpool and where there are horses there are always myriads of flies to carry dysentery. Our milkman kept his cows in a shippen at the back of his dairy, but fortunately in summer for part of the time they grazed outside the city, and took their quota of flies with them.

Hens and pigeons were common in back yards. Men kept fighting-cocks, though this was illegal, and many were the bloody battles in the long summer evenings on which men wagered a large portion of their public assistance money.

Much of this the younger children were able to accept as a way of life as they slowly forgot their earlier life, though Tony once said to me earnestly as I bathed a grazed knee he had acquired while playing rounders in the street, 'I don't like the kind of life we live, Helen, and when I grow big I shall change it.'

'I hope you will,' I replied equally gravely. 'You've got brains and you could get a scholarship to a better school – and that would get you out of it.'

'Why don't you go to school, Helen?'

The tears, never far from my myopic eyes, sprang up. I bent my head so that he could not see them. 'Mother needs me at home, dear.'

'How will you get out of it then?'

'I really don't know.' I made myself sound cheerful, as I carefully dried the small wound because wounds seemed to go septic so fast. 'When Daddy gets a job, things will change a lot.'

He stood up and stretched his thin little body. 'Perhaps you will marry a prince,' he suggested hopefully.

'Perhaps,' I agreed, though I knew that girls as ugly as I who also wore spectacles did not stand a chance of matrimony; my mother had always indicated that such was the case and I think I had already been written off as a future maiden aunt. This did not stop me, however, from dreaming for the rest of the afternoon that I married the beautiful, humane and exciting Edward, Prince of Wales.

Tony and Brian also had a dream world of their own. They rarely quarrelled and, with Fiona, they played highly imaginative games in which they sailed the world – Brian always fell overboard and was rescued by Tony – or drove trains and cars which had innumerable comic accidents.

Playing in the open, even if the air was polluted, made them more hungry and it was impossible to satisfy them. If we were to cook anything, we still had to buy coal, so that summer expenses were much the same as winter ones.

We approached our second winter in Liverpool with undisguised dread. We had commenced the first bitter January there with one set of good winter clothing apiece and two blankets. Now, not one of us had a whole garment or a pair of shoes without holes in them. Indeed, four of us were reduced to ragged running-shoes or nothing at all on our feet.

My father was a pitiful sight even in comparison with the ragged crew who lined up with him for public assistance. His elbows stuck through the sleeves of what had once been a tweed jacket and his knees were equally naked. He had no socks and there was very little left of his shirt. He used to thread the remains of his old school tie through the torn collar and knot it, in the mistaken belief that nobody would notice the bare chest underneath it. His underwear had, like that of the rest of the family, worn out, its life shortened by inadequate laundering. His chest was red from being chapped by the wind; but he suffered most from pain in his hands.

Both hands had been badly frost-bitten during his military service in Russia, and, on the hospital ship which brought him home, the surgeons had debated whether or not they should be amputated. The wonderful care he received, however, saved him from this; but intensely cold weather turned them white, and I used to sit and massage them to revive the circulation. It was then that they became most painful.

One freezing November day, urged on by two shipping clerks shivering with him in one of the endless queues in which he spent most of his life, he applied to the relieving officer of the public assistance committee for help to buy a pair of shoes and a pair of gloves.

Clothing, he was told tartly, was given in kind and stamped with the initials of the public assistance committee, so that it could not be sold or pawned.

'I don't mind what it is stamped with,' replied Father humbly, 'as long as it lessens the pain in my hands.'

His case file was sent for and examined.

'You are not eligible for help with clothing,' was the verdict. 'You do not come under the jurisdiction of Liverpool.'

The same old problem. We were not from Liverpool. Our rate of public assistance was that given in the small town from which we came, and the sum was collected from that town by Liverpool. We got none of the little extras such as money for winter coal or for Christmas which Liverpool struggled to give its less fortunate citizens, nor were we eligible for clothing.

'What shall I do?' my father cried, in despair.

'Try one of the voluntary agencies.'

So Father got the run-around as it was sometimes called. He was sent from agency to agency. And they all said they could not help, because he was drawing public assistance and could get boots from that committee. In vain, he explained that the town from which we had come did not give clothing and we were ineligible for help from Liverpool.

One agency offered second-hand boots at a very reduced price, but any price was too high for us to pay. We had once spent three shillings in a secondhand clothes shop in an effort to make my mother presentable again, feeling that she had the better chance of employment, and had had to reduce our meagre food intake to a dangerous level, in consequence. If it had not been for our kind policeman's pint of milk, Edward would have surely died that week.

Then Mother suddenly got a job 'on commission only'. She was to sell radios from door to door.

Up and down the better-class streets she tramped, knocking at each door and trying to beguile reluctant housewives into agreeing to a demonstration of the radio in their homes. On the third day, she did find a woman willing to listen to her, and it was agreed that the radio would be brought that night for her husband to see.

The demonstration radio, meanwhile, was delivered to the door of our house by a supervisor, and was taken in by Miss Sinford, the most presentable of all the inhabitants.

'Helen!' she shrieked up the stairs to me. 'Come and remove this wicked temptation from the hall!'

I ran down the stairs with Edward on my hip.

Miss Sinford pointed an accusing finger at a cardboard box and a wet battery beside it. The box was clearly marked that it contained a radio, and I guessed that it had been delivered in connection with Mother's new job.

'Thank you, Miss Sinford.'

I sat Edward down on the grubby hall runner, and Miss Sinford withdrew with one of her loudest sniffs of disapproval. Avril had followed me down, and I left her to mind Edward while I puffed my way upstairs again with the radio. I made a second journey for the wet battery and carried it up so fast that I splashed some of the acid on my bare legs, burning them painfully.

A third journey was made to retrieve Edward and Avril.

Still panting from the journeys up and down, I

read the instructions on the outside of the box to Avril, and then very carefully unpacked the radio and put it on the table. I plugged in the wet and dry batteries and nervously turned one of the knobs. The shining newness of it awed us both.

Suddenly the room was filled with the sweet sound of violins.

Avril climbed up on to one of the chairs and put her head close to the speaker and Edward smiled and sucked his thumb. I stood in ecstasy while the music swept round me.

We spent a blissful afternoon listening to a faraway world where people spoke as we did and music was part of life.

My parents were extremely angry when they came home and found the radio unpacked and working.

'It does not belong to us,' said my mother furiously. 'You know quite well that you are not to touch anything which does not belong to you.'

'I haven't harmed it,' I said defiantly.

'No, she has not,' interrupted Avril aggressively. 'And I heard a nice lady say "happy birthday" and "hello, twins" on Children's Hour and I liked it.'

'Well,' said Father, turning it off firmly. 'Don't touch it again.'

Mother said, 'I have to demonstrate it tonight, to Mr and Mrs Smithers, and I don't know how to do it.'

'You just put these plugs in here, like Helen did, and you turn that knob there,' instructed Avril, stabbing the appropriate plugs and knob with a grubby finger. 'And it goes.'

She looked up at my mother with hard blue eyes, as if daring her to say she was not right.

Father smiled.

'She is right, you know. That is all you have to do.' He looked worried. 'I suppose the supervisor will move the thing to the Smithers' house for you in his car?'

'Heavens, no. I have to take it myself.'

'But you can't carry that weight,' we said in chorus.

'Besides,' I added, sadly surveying the burning marks on my grey legs, 'the acid from the wet battery can splash and burn your stockings.'

We all knew that without stockings Mother was not suitably dressed for work, and we had all observed that even if she was not much interested in us, she was more alive, more aware of things going on around her, when looking for work.

Silence fell upon the family. The radio and its

batteries were really too awkward for anyone to carry any distance.

Tony, who had been playing one of his endless games of puffer-trains with a dead cinder from the fireplace, looked up, as he shunted his imaginary train into an imaginary siding, and said quietly, 'Put it in the Chariot and wheel it round to the lady's house.'

We all burst out laughing, and I snatched Edward out of the pram.

'Try it for size,' I invited.

Very carefully, the radio was put back into its box and lowered into the stinking pram. The batteries followed. It all fitted in.

A gentle sigh of relief went through the family.

We ate a hasty meal of boiled potatoes, which tasted strongly of the smoke from an old shoe I had picked up in the street and brought home for fuel. Then, since it was dark, the whole family went in procession behind Father, who carefully wheeled the Chariot with its unusual contents. I clutched Edward to me and brought up the rear.

Down the street under the light of the gas-lamps we marched, past the brothels, past the garish lights and conversational roar of the local pub, past the boys lounging at the street corners, who watched the weird procession speculatively, out of the slum which was our world, into quieter streets of neat terrace housing.

At a corner, out of sight of the home of Mother's customer, we unloaded the radio and set it down on the pavement. We whispered conspiratorially together, trying to decide how to get it to the house concerned, without the customer seeing any of us except Mother.

Father finally decided that he would make the first sortie and carry the batteries to the front step of the customer's house which led straight on to the pavement; there was no front yard or garden to be negotiated.

We watched with excited anticipation as he glided ghostlike down the empty street, quickly deposited the batteries, and continued on down the street, round the block and back to us, so that he actually passed the house only once. Then Alan and Mother together carried the radio itself to the house, and put it down on the step. Mother stood by it, while Alan fled down the street, taking the same course as Father had.

Mother was out of sight of all of us, but we heard the peal of the old-fashioned front door bell when she rang it; and the sounds of the door opening and shutting and of strong Lancashire voices came to us clearly through the frosty air.

Brian and Tony started an excited conversation. Father hushed them immediately. He was standing tense, listening like a hound.

My arms were aching with Edward's weight, so I put him into the pram. Avril complained that she was cold and I put her in with him and rubbed her legs which were mottled like an old woman's from exposure.

Coatless, hatless and hungry, we were all shivering by the time we heard the sound of the door opening again and cheerful voices bidding Mother 'good night'.

She was coming slowly towards us. In the gas-light, her face had a look of stupefied wonderment, as if she had just experienced a religious revelation of some kind.

The policeman on the beat was coming slowly towards us, trying the doors of each shop which faced the road on which we stood; and Father, ever fearful of being arrested for vagrancy, moved us slowly to meet Mother.

'I sold it – that very one – they wanted the demonstration model. They signed the hire purchase agreement and gave me the deposit there and then. And they gave me tea and cake.' Her voice quivered, as she mentioned the last item.

'Really?' exclaimed Father, unable to believe

that in Depression-bound Liverpool anybody could afford to buy anything. 'Are you sure?'

'Yes,' she whispered, sudden pride in her voice.

'What will you get for it? Your commission?'

'Thirty shillings.'

'We shall have to tell the public assistance committee. The little bit you earned selling treacle was not worth worrying about. We shall have to declare thirty shillings – and they will just cut it off our allowance.' Father's voice was tired and old.

'Are you mad?' cried Mother with an unexpected burst of spirit.

'No, of course not. But it is not honest not to tell them.'

'We will not tell them,' said Mother savagely. 'They'd let us die. They don't care. Why should we bother about what is honest and what is not?' The bitter question sounded all the more so because it was expressed in her beautiful contralto voice, a voice almost identical to Brian's.

Father had his arms crossed over his chest and his hands tucked into his armpits to keep them warm. He said in a broken voice, 'I must have some gloves. I can't bear the pain in my hands any more.'

'And I must have lots of fish and chips,' shouted Avril unexpectedly. 'Lots of lovely fish and chips.'

Fiona clutched my arm.

'Helen, I feel awfully odd.' Her face was ashen.

I caught her as she fainted. She was the quietest, most uncomplaining of us all and, as I held her frail little frame in my arms and looked down at her closed eyes with lashes like Michaelmas daisies, it seemed as if Death was breathing down the back of my neck.

'Fish and chips,' roared Avril again, quite unperturbed by her sister's collapse.

CHAPTER TWENTY

Mother never sold another radio. It did teach her, however, that she might be able to sell things. Even her dismissal a week later because of her lack of sales did not deter her, and a little while later she got a temporary job in a store demonstrating baby baths. The store was gloriously warm, and she spent her days bathing a doll and extolling the virtues of rubber baths to expectant mothers who came to buy layettes in the baby-wear department. An arduous week's bathing netted her ten shillings in commission, which she spent on shoes and stockings for herself, necessities if she was to continue to try for work.

Christmas loomed near. I did not mention it to Avril or Edward. The other children whispered to each other about it. None of them was in the

Christmas play the school was producing and it was clear that none of them had any hope of our being able to celebrate the birth of Christ.

On Christmas Eve, we were all seated in our living-room. The only light was a shaft of moonlight across the floor. We had a small stub of candle and a couple of matches to be used in emergency and these lay ready on the mantelpiece. Outside the church bells were ringing for Christmas services, and across the road in the mysterious house doors slammed occasionally and rowdy voices rose and fell upon the still air.

I had just decided that Edward, Avril and Tony should go to bed, when Mrs Foster's genteel bass could be heard in the lower hall.

'A parcel has come for the top floor. Please come and collect it!'

We were all immediately galvanized into action, except Mother, who continued to sit with her head leaning against the window-frame staring out of the window. We clattered like an army down the myriad of stairs into the hallway, which was dimly lit by a single gas jet.

'Wow!' exclaimed Tony.

It was a very large parcel, addressed to Father, and it took the combined strength of Father, Alan and me to carry it up to our top-floor rooms.

We placed it reverently on the dirty table, and, with shaking hands, Father fumbled with the knots of twine, trying to open it. Finally, he gave up, and we tore at the brown paper and the corrugated cardboard box underneath, frantically trying to find the contents.

We clawed at straw and the infuriating string, and suddenly a golden orange rolled out, sailed slowly across the table and fell with a juicy plonk on to the floor.

An *orange*! An exquisitely perfumed, golden fruit was sitting right in the middle of our floor.

We all gaped at it, and then renewed our frenzied opening up of the package, while Edward crawled across to look at the strange object which had fallen off the table.

We disinterred a turkey of proportions generous enough to have pleased a king, a large plum pudding in a bowl, a bag of potatoes, more oranges, and a box of sweets. Sweets! We were nearly hysterical with excitement.

We had heard of these Christmas parcels, though we had not expected to be the recipients of one; there had been considerable controversy about them in the columns of the *Liverpool Echo.* Many people held that it was ridiculous to help the poor only at Christmas, that the money spent could be put to better uses throughout the year. Whoever made up the parcel for us, however, would have been amply rewarded by the ecstasy with which we received it. It was too much for me, and I burst into tears.

All this time, Mother had continued to sit with her head against the window-frame, though she had shown some interest at first. Suddenly she began to laugh in a high-pitched, wild fashion.

We were silenced immediately. My father was trembling visibly, as he looked at her. Was this the breakdown he had been fearing?

'How are we going to cook it?' she screamed between gusts of laughter. 'With no fire, no oven, no nothing!'

'Be quiet!' Father said firmly, trying to keep a grip on the situation.

Edward and Avril began to cry. Brian stood, an orange in his hand, as if turned to stone. Fiona, clutching the tattered remains of her doll, moved closer to Alan, who put his arm protectively round her shoulder. The darkness of the room made the whole scene macabre and unreal.

Tony, who had been about to open the box of sweets, said, 'Listen!'

Through Mother's wild laughter could be heard

the sound of a heavy tread on the top staircase leading to our landing.

'Mrs Foster,' muttered Brian, his voice full of dread. 'Have we paid our rent?'

Avril stopped crying and listened: 'Mr Parish,' she suggested.

The thought of the public assistance committee's visitor discovering that we had a secret hoard of turkey and oranges and deducting its value from our miserable weekly pittance made me frantic, and I ran to the door with the idea of stopping his entering.

I was too late.

A knock sounded on our door.

Mother was still giggling to herself and Father seemed unable to move.

I will be brave. I will be polite, I told myself, and opened the door.

A huge, joint sigh of relief nearly blew the visitor back down the stairs.

'Ah come,' said the visitor, peering round in the gloom, 'to wish yer all a Happy Christmas from Mr Hicks and meself.'

'Mrs Hicks!' exclaimed Brian, and flew to his dear friend from the basement. She caught him in her one free arm.

'Well, now me little peacock! How's our Brian?'

Father came out of his trance and led her through the darkness to our second chair. She sat down and carefully arranged her skirts over it like Queen Victoria about to be photographed.

Mother was quietened by this unexpected visitor and regarded her with silent dislike. Mother, as far as possible, never spoke to anyone in the house, except Mrs Foster, and regarded all our neighbours with abhorrence. Her chilling stare did nothing to cool Mrs Hicks's exuberance. She carefully laid a paper shopping-bag on the floor in front of her, and one by one she brought out a little package for each child and for Father. Lastly, she brought one out for Mother.

'Here yer are, luv. Happy Christmas to yez.'

Mother just stared.

'Come on, luv. It won't always be like this. Maybe the New Year'll bring some luck to yez.'

I could see my mother fighting to make a tremendous effort, and, at last, in a little, panting voice, she said, 'Thank you, Mrs Hicks. You are very kind. I heartily reciprocate your good wishes.' She took the parcel and laid it in her lap.

Mrs Hicks was obviously nonplussed by the word 'reciprocate' but she beamed at Mother in a maternally approving way, and said, 'Na, that's better. You'll soon be well, luv.'

'Helen, can we open them? Please!' Fiona had forgotten her earlier fright and was entranced at having a present.

I looked at Father and he said, 'Yes, of course.'

We all tore at the crumpled, old tissue paper of our parcels.

Mrs Hicks had knitted each of us a pair of gloves and each pair had a distinguishing Fair Isle pattern in a contrasting colour worked into it.

'So as you will know whose is which,' she explained. 'Ah made 'em outta a couple of old pullovers ah bought at Maurrie's.'

I looked at her with wonderment. Such an enterprising idea had never occurred to me. The idea was better than the Christmas present itself, for I could knit. Grandma had taught me. Mrs Hicks was brilliant! Bits of old hand-knitted sweaters and cardigans, too holey to be sold as complete garments, could be bought from old Maurrie at the second-hand clothing store for as little as two for a penny. I could buy some, unravel them and knit, just as old Mrs Hicks had done. Edward could have a warm sweater. I forgot my earlier tears in the splendour of this new idea.

Mrs Hicks meantime had grown accustomed to the darkness and spotted the turkey on the table.

'Got a Christmas parcel, have yer? Proper nice, ain't it?'

Father agreed that it was proper nice. Mother stared emptily at the naked bird.

'There is one difficulty,' said Father.

Mrs Hicks looked puzzled.

'We haven't got an oven to cook it in,' and he added rather apologetically, 'or a knife to cut it up small enough to stew on our fireplace.'

'We haven't even got a fire,' said Alan.

'Oh aye,' responded Mrs Hicks. 'Now that's a bit of a difficulty, aint it?' She ran her red hands up and down her ample thighs while she considered the matter.

'Tell yer what. Ah'll be cooking me own turkey on the morning, but there's a good fire going downstairs now. If I turn it to the oven you could cook yours now. It would be cooked afore midnight, when we goes to bed.'

'Oh, Mrs Hicks!' I burst out. 'That would be marvellous.'

Father looked dimly hopeful.

'Would you mind?' he asked.

She laughed at him. 'Not a bit. You could put some potatoes round it, to bake, and you'd have a reet good meal.' She looked at our dead fireplace, and added, 'You can put the pudding at the back o' me fire at the same time. Most o' the heat's only going up t' chimney right now.'

Mother said suddenly, 'Thank you, Mrs Hicks.' I thought for a horrid minute that she was going to follow it with 'But we do not require your assistance'. She controlled herself, however, when the whole family, sensing this, turned on her in frozen, silent rage.

While the children sucked the oranges, Father and I took the bird, the pudding and the potatoes downstairs.

Mrs Hicks put it into a baking-tin which was thick with the encrustations of twenty-five years of cooking, and larded it with a bit of bacon fat. Then, guided by her instructions, Father laid it in the ancient oven to the side of the kitchen fire. Some potatoes followed and the heavy, iron door was swung shut, Mrs Hicks having carefully checked that the cat, who apparently slept there normally, was not inside behind the turkey. Mr Hicks grinned all over his little, ferrety face and promised to sit and watch that it did not burn and to add water as needed to the blackened saucepan into which the pudding was subsequently lowered.

'One of yez come down in three hours' time,' commanded Mrs Hicks, poking up the fire with a large iron poker. 'Ah reckon it'll be done by then.

You could wrap it in a blanket and it'll keep a bit warm till tomorrer.'

Joy gave strength to our weakened legs and we ran all the way up the stairs, to sink, half fainting, upon the floor when we got to the top.

Nobody could bear to be put to bed, so we sat around in the dim light from the moon and the street, until the closing of the nearby public house told us it was ten o'clock. After that we took it in turns to count up to sixty, so as to make a rough estimate of thirty minutes more, at the end of which Alan and I bolted down to the basement.

We knocked and entered the vast cavern which had been the kitchen when the house was built. Our bare feet pattered on the old brick tiles as we crossed to the fireplace in response to Mr Hicks's invitation to come and get warm. He was just lifting the pudding saucepan from the hob. His wife took it from him and carried it across to the sandstone sink in the corner. With a skilful twist she got the pudding out without scalding herself, and set it on the bare wooden table, which I noticed with surprise was scrubbed almost pure white. She spread a newspaper on another corner and went to the oven to get the turkey.

Immediately she unlatched the heavy door a heavenly aroma flooded the room, drowning out the usual odours of damp, pine disinfectant and unwashed winter clothes. Saliva ran from my mouth and I hastily brushed it away.

'Ah think it's cooked,' she said, twisting one of the bird's legs with expert fingers. 'Are yer goin' to carry it oop like it is?'

We had few plates and none big enough to hold a turkey, so I said that we would carry it up in the meat-tin and bring the receptacle back in the morning, early enough for her to cook her own Christmas dinner in it. I did not tell her that I could not bear, in any case, to part with a single drop of the fat in the pan.

She agreed to this cheerfully, wrapped up the baked potatoes in a newspaper, then told us to wait a moment, while she rummaged in the back of her dusty kitchen dresser.

'Here yer are,' she said triumphantly. 'Here's a bit o' candle to light you up them stairs.'

She lit the small candle stub she had found and presented it to Alan, gave me two crumpled sheets of newspaper so that I would not burn my hands while carrying the hot meat-tin, and sent us upstairs again.

'Gosh, the pudding feels lovely and hot,' exclaimed Alan, as he staggered up with the paper parcels of pudding and potatoes.

The family, except for Mother, was gathered to greet us on the top landing, and a great oooh sounded at the sight of the turkey, as we mounted the last flight.

'I'll wrap it in the newspaper I carried it with,' I said firmly. 'Perhaps it will keep it a little warm till tomorrow.'

I could see Father's Adam's apple bob in the candlelight, as he swallowed; and hope died on the children's faces.

Avril kicked my shin to draw my attention to her.

'I want to eat mine now,' she said determinedly.

Tony's eyes looked enormous in his death's head face.

Again the saliva gathered in my mouth, but I said, 'It's not Christmas until tomorrow.'

'To hell with Christmas,' said Alan bitterly.

An hour later, there was only a white skeleton left, scraped clean by small clawing hands and teeth. Even Mother came alive, after devouring nearly a whole leg with the gulping enthusiasm of an ex-prisoner of war. We ate the baked potatoes, skin and all, we ate the sweets and pudding, every scrap.

We slept.

CHAPTER TWENTY-ONE

Malnutrition, when much prolonged, causes a terrible apathy, an inability to concentrate or think constructively, and that winter was so grim that my mind was closed to the intense suffering of my parents. A child's world is a small one and given a reasonable round of home and school, his life is fairly full. Our little ones suffered unbelievably, however, as they dragged themselves to and from school through snow and rain. Even brave Alan cried when the great chilblains on his heels burst and went septic, and it seemed as if the clothes of all of them were permanently wet; good fires are a necessity in a climate as rainy as Lancashire's. In my parents' case, however, they suffered not only all that we did but also from social deprivation; they starved mentally as well as physically.

To me, the suffering of Fiona and baby Edward was the more scarifying, because it was silent. Fiona never complained as the others did; she sat quiet and terrified in a kind of mental burrow like a fox that has been savaged by hounds and must be quiet lest they find him again; only when she was playing with Brian and Tony did a happier little girl emerge. And I loved her so much that it filled me with grief to be unable to comfort her – she was past comforting. Edward, who could now crawl rapidly and occasionally stood up, was making valiant efforts to speak. He seemed to have a natural serenity, but when he cried (which he rarely did), it was with terrible deep sobs that came slowly, not at all like Avril's ferocious bellows when she was thwarted in any way.

Until hunger made him fall into lethargy, my father tried to pick the brains of other men who stood with him in the endless queues. He tried to find out how they stayed alive and how they hoped to get a job. But, finally, it took all his strength to get to the labour exchange or to the offices of the public assistance committee and stand, without fainting, until he received a curt 'nothing today' from the former and forty-three shillings each Thursday from the latter.

We always had colds. Old copies of the *Liverpool*

Echo were collected from anywhere we could find them and torn up for use as handkerchiefs. The paper was then used to make a fire in the tiny bedroom fireplace in our living-room.

The acid which I had spilled on my leg from the battery of the radio caused a burn which went septic, and the sore showed signs of spreading. Old Miss Sinford noticed the mark on my leg as I went upstairs one day and commanded that I come into her room to have it examined. She sat me down on a wooden chair placed on a piece of newspaper and, having put on a pair of gold-rimmed spectacles, she took a good look at it.

'I'll poultice it for you,' she decided. 'You should have kept it cleaner.'

The fact that I was seated in the middle of a newspaper indicated that she knew how dirty our family was, so I just smiled weakly.

She found a clean piece of white cloth, put it in an old sugar basin and poured over it boiling water from the kettle on the hob. She then wrung it out and slapped it on to the sore, scalding the surrounding flesh until I clutched Edward too hard and he cried out. She hurled texts about Good Samaritans at me, as she worked with trembly ancient fingers, and then ordered me down to her room the next morning for a repeat performance.

Her room was spotless, filled with crochet work which she had done herself. In the window on a wickerwork table stood a large aspidistra in a plum-coloured china pot, and I gathered that an aspidistra was a lot of work, as she felt the need to dust it daily. She cooked at the fireplace, which was larger than ours, her room having been the dining-room of the original home.

It was from her that I learned that the house opposite, which was visited by so many seamen, was a House of Sin and that the women who lived in it were harlots. 'Harlot' was a word which occurred in the Bible, so I ventured to ask her what it meant.

She blinked at me through her spectacles, as if realizing for the first time how young and innocent I was. Then she pointed a bony finger at me and said sharply, 'Girls should not ask such questions.' Her voice became shrill. 'It is not a word I should have used. It is a word you must not use. Out! I must pray!'

She seized me by the shoulder, turned me about and pushed me into the hall.

Bewildered, I took myself back upstairs and left my leg to heal by itself, which it eventually did.

Next time I went to the library, I looked up the offending word. It really sounded very wicked indeed, and I was most impressed.

Fiona came home from school one day, in tears. She said she had a pain in her back and chest. I felt her forehead. It was burning with heat. Helplessly, I looked at her and we were both terribly afraid.

When Father came home from the library, I told him about Fiona. I had laid her on the bed and, to keep her warm, had covered her with what few odds and ends of blanket and garments I could find.

We went to look at her and found that she had tossed aside her wrappings and was muttering feverishly, her mouselike hands clenching and unclenching.

Father clamped his mouth tight. His breath came in small gasps and perspiration glistened on his forehead.

Alan came softly up to us.

'Don't you think we had better send for the doctor, Daddy?' he asked.

'I haven't any money to pay him,' was the despairing response.

'We could tell him that.' Alan's lips trembled. Like all of us, he loved Fiona. 'He might come anyway.'

I said, 'We have nothing to lose by asking. Is Fiona very ill, Daddy?'

'Yes,' he replied. 'I can see that she is very ill indeed – I am not sure what it is, though.'

I leaned over Fiona and whispered that we would get a doctor for her and she would soon be better.

'I'll go and ask,' said Alan in his bravest voice, sticking his chest out and trying to look strong.

'Yes, do so. I think Helen and I had better stay here. I haven't any paper on which to write a letter. You will have to explain to him yourself. Tell him about the pain and the temperature.'

Tony, Brian and Avril tiptoed into the room and went silently out again.

Alan plunged out into the February wind once more. Terrified of facing whoever would answer the doctor's door but even more terrified about Fiona's illness, he seized the doctor's brass knocker and banged it.

The door was answered by a neatly dressed older woman.

'The doctor's out,' she said before Alan could open his mouth.

'It's my sister,' said Alan. 'She's awfully ill and we haven't any money to pay the doctor. But, please, will he come?'

The boy's evident fear made the woman soften her tone.

'Well,' she said, 'step in, lad. I am not sure that the doctor can come. He's very busy.'

Alan, shivering, stepped into the linoleumed hall. Under the faint light of a very low wattage electric light bulb, the lady surveyed him.

She sighed at what she saw, and took down a notebook from beside a telephone on the hall wall. 'Tell me your name and address and I'll ask him. Now then.'

Alan told her, and explained the symptoms of the illness as best he could.

'Now mind,' said his questioner as she shut the notebook. 'I don't know whether the doctor can come. I'll have to ask him. If he does come, it will be after surgery, about half past nine.'

The hours dragged by. We took it in turns to sit by Fiona. She would not take the tea we offered her. I wetted our only towel which was, as usual, very dirty, and wiped her face and hands with cold water. This seemed to console her a little. Occasionally, she was racked by coughing.

Mother came home and stared dumbly at her second daughter. It was as if she could not let any more troubles in upon herself; she seemed numbed, unable to accept any more. Her unkempt hair had escaped from her hat and hung in straggling oily tails down to her shoulders. Her hands were swollen with chilblains, in spite of Mrs Hicks's gloves, and she stood awkwardly, because the heels of her shoes were worn down so badly that she walked almost as if she was bandy-legged.

'We must keep her covered,' she said at last.

It was difficult to see in the reflected light from the street lamp, and Father said worriedly, 'I don't know how the doctor is going to be able to see to examine her – if he comes.'

'Couldn't we borrow a shilling to put in the electric meter?' I asked.

'Brian went down and tried the couple below; they didn't have one. I can't ask Mrs Foster – we still owe her a week's rent – and I can't ask Mrs Hicks because I haven't yet paid her back the last shilling I borrowed.'

This was the first intimation I had had of his borrowing from the other tenants; it accounted for a general coldness towards us recently.

Without a watch it was difficult to tell the time, but both house and street were quiet when the front door bell rang. Hopefully, Brian pounded down the stairs to open the door.

A firm voice said, 'We can't afford to fall down this black pit – I'll put my flashlight on.'

Brian laughed shrilly and called, 'Daddy, Daddy, Helen! The doctor has come!'

The bedroom door opened and the light of a torch blinded me momentarily. The doctor must have had long experience of the straits of poverty to carry such a powerful torch.

'Come in, come in,' said Father, his voice filled with relief.

I stood up respectfully as the doctor put down his bag.

'Now, what have we here?' he asked as he got out his stethoscope, and then took Fiona's wrist in long, capable fingers.

Father explained the symptoms and I nearly stopped breathing as the doctor listened to his patient's labouring lungs and frequent coughing.

'Pleurisy, I think,' he said. 'She must have hospital treatment immediately. I will go and telephone the Children's Sanatorium, and arrange for an ambulance.'

Father whispered, 'It isn't tuberculosis, is it?' In those days, tuberculosis was still a major killer.

'I doubt it. The hospital will take X-rays.' He stood looking down at Fiona's face by the light of the torch. 'Does she have a mother?'

'Yes,' Father replied. 'You kindly took some stitches out for her after an abdominal operation some time ago.'

'Oh, did I,' he said absently, and then rather

more alertly, 'Yes, I remember. How is she?'

Father looked uneasily at me, and then plunged in. 'Her physical health has improved – as far as it can in our circumstances.' He paused, and then added, 'She isn't herself, though.'

The doctor nodded understandingly. He did not offer any more help. He would deal with our emergency; he could not do more. He had to treat first those patients who could pay. In the torchlight I could see the frayed cuffs of his overcoat and I guessed that he had very little himself.

The doctor asked to see Mother, who had been up in the attic room dealing with Tony. Tony had had a nightmare and had woken up screaming.

When she came, he instructed her to get Fiona ready for hospital.

Mother said in a flat tone of voice, 'There is nothing to do. She must go as she is. She has no other garments than those she has on – and I cannot wash her in cold water in her present state.'

So Fiona went to a huge hospital on the farther outskirts of the city, without benefit of bath, toothbrush or nightgown, and my poor, crushed mother suffered the indignity of seeing her almost unconscious child stripped of her clothes and plunged into a disinfecting bath, her head rolling on her neck as the probationers washed her crawling hair. The tattered clothes were rolled into a bundle and handed to Mother, with the curt information that she could wait.

Mother was used to waiting – she spent her days in office and shop waiting-rooms as she applied for job after job with hordes of other applicants. Finally, about three in the morning a night nurse remembered that she was still there and told her she could go.

'I want to know what is the matter with the child and I want to see her, now she is in bed.'

'You will have to come on visiting days. Your doctor will be informed regarding her illness, and he will tell you.'

My mother lifted her hand to slap this inhuman automaton, but she was afraid of what might happen to Fiona if she made a fuss of any kind, so she turned slowly into the long, brown corridor to the front door.

She had come to the hospital with Fiona in the ambulance. Nobody had considered how she was to get home again. Outside was the dark and bitter cold of a February night.

She paused on the step, shaken by the knowledge that the only way to get home was to walk the seven miles to our part of the city. She was not even sure of the route.

The city was completely quiet and, emboldened by this, she set out, following the tram lines which glimmered in the gaslight. The freezing wind cut into her and, after a couple of miles, she was so cold that she was staggering in a ragged line along the pavement.

A dim light at a corner attracted her attention. It was a telephone box, and she quickened her step and sought refuge inside it.

Paralysed with cold, she stood there looking dully at the receiver on its hook, the telephone book hanging below it, and at two buttons marked 'A' and 'B'. Idly, she read the instructions for making a call.

'Insert two pennies. When the telephone is answered press Button A. If no reply, press button B for the return of the twopence.'

Return of the twopence!

She hopefully pressed Button B.

Nothing happened, so, after a few minutes, she started again on her long hike homewards. An early tram rumbled past her, its lights flashing as it pitched and tossed its way along the lines.

When she reached the next public telephone box, she entered it and, without much hope, pressed Button B, and was immediately rewarded by the happy rattle of two falling pennies. She snatched them up and took the next tram home.

Father and I had waited up for her and were frantic with anxiety. Our anxiety turned to fury when we heard of the discourteous treatment she had received, and we did our best to comfort her before managing to get her to go to bed.

Our visits to the sanatorium were strictly regulated by whether we could find a telephone box where someone had forgotten to press Button B for the return of their twopence – and it was remarkable how many we found.

Though Fiona's illness was long and our public assistance was reduced by the amount given for her maintenance, we were not altogether sorry. She was at least fed in hospital – great hunks of bread and margarine, bowls of sugarless porridge, meat stews, boiled puddings and steamed fish. Patients were expected to augment the hospital's food by supplying their own sugar, jam, cake and fruit. We had nothing to bring Fiona. The diet was, however, so much better than she had received for many a month that, once the pleurisy was drained, she began to look much stronger.

She was sorely troubled by bugs in the hospital

bed. Father complained, and was told roughly that she must have brought them in with her.

'She was stripped and bathed when she came in,' he said. 'Perhaps the bed could be stoved.'

A ferocious female, who looked as if she had been put through a starch solution with her uniform, said cruelly, 'Of course, it will be stoved – after your child is discharged.'

Father's expression, after that remark, was like that in the painting of Christ crucified which hung over my grandmother's bed. He bowed his head and turned silently away.

A slightly plumper waif of a child was returned to us six weeks later. There was no ambulance this time and she found the long tram ride a sore trial. She came home to again face hunger and cold with us.

'The spring is coming,' we comforted her.

The studied rudeness with which every member of the family was faced whenever dealing with officialdom, as personified by the public assistance committee, by the labour exchanges, by the voluntary agencies working in the city, was a revelation to us. We began to understand, as never before, the great gulf between rich and poor, between middle class and labour. It considerably improved our manners towards our less fortunate neighbours.

When I grew up, I told myself, I would do some kind of work which would improve this situation and make it possible for people to be helped without at the same time humiliating them.

When I grew up!

But I was growing up. Even in my pinched body, changes were taking place which indicated that soon I would be a young woman. A ghastly, ugly, uneducated wreck of a young woman but still a woman.

As I sat on the doorstep in the weak April sunshine, Edward on my knee, I wondered what would become of me. Other girls went to school and then to work, but for me life had stopped in one place on my first day in Liverpool. The other children were getting at least a basic education; Alan talked hopefully of Tony and Brian being able to win scholarships to grammar school; he himself was too old to sit the examination, but he worked hard at school and read a lot afterwards. At fourteen, he could leave school and he hoped to get a job 'with a future'. Fiona, I thought, would sooner or later marry well – she was so pretty; I did not consider how, in this wilderness of slum, she would manage to do that.

Avril, throwing her weight about both physically and verbally, amongst a number of small girls from neighbouring houses, was tough enough to take care of herself, and Edward, watching the world go by from the safe refuge of my lap, was young enough not to have to worry.

Without an education, I saw myself being kept at home until my parents died and then becoming some bad-tempered old lady's companion-help, subject always to the whims and fancies of others. I knew I was far too plain ever to hope for marriage.

I laid my cheek on little Edward's scurvy head and decided that such a life was not worth living.

CHAPTER TWENTY-TWO

Encouraged by the friendly old gentleman on the park bench, I continued to read. When I explained to him that I ought to be in school, he said firmly and wisely that it was my parents' responsibility. He pointed out that, in studying by myself, I was following in the footsteps of many great Lancastrians, who, though doomed to poverty because they were weavers and caught up in the industrial revolution, found means to study and outshine their better-educated contemporaries. He cited the examples of John Butterworth, the mathematician from Haggate, who never earned more than fifteen shillings a week and learned to read and write at the age of twenty. Such was his love of learning that he became one of the finest geometricians of his day; and James Crowther and Richard Buxton, the

Manchester botanists, both self-taught, both always poor, both famous.

I sighed. There was no help there. I wanted to eat and be warm every day of my life.

Avril and I had discovered one beautifully warm spot in Liverpool, although it was rather a long way from home. Sefton Park had a fine glass palm-house, which was kept at tropical temperatures to encourage the growth of the palms and similar plants inside. Avril, Edward and I used to go into it often and crawl under the great creepers to get warm, emerging later with our bottoms covered with earth, damper but warmer.

Once we were discovered by two earnest young men carrying notebooks and pencils. They were wreathed around with long scarves in the colours of the university, and when they found us they were at first puzzled and then amused.

Avril and I stared at them like a pair of scared rabbits.

'Hide and seek?' one young man inquired.

I nodded assent, and, like fellow conspirators, they rearranged the foliage over us and tiptoed away. A gardener on another occasion was not so kind.

'We don't want no dirty ragamuffins in here,' he shouted, and sent us packing.

Crestfallen, we stalked out of the glass house with what dignity we could muster, and I pushed the Chariot homeward, passing through a working-class shopping street on the way.

Halfway up the street, I came to a large, red brick building surrounded by a matching brick wall. It was an elementary school, silent and deserted because it was Saturday. I was about to pass it without much interest, when the remains of a poster flapping in the wind caught my attention. It announced the opening of evening school the previous September. Courses in commercial arithmetic, bookkeeping, English, shorthand and several other subjects were offered.

I stopped.

I had never heard of evening school and I could hardly believe that one could go to school outside the normal hours. I could have skipped for joy.

I wondered if one could enroll at times other than September. Perhaps there would be someone on the premises who could tell me about it. I wheeled the Chariot through the gate leading to the school yard and was hesitantly moving round the building searching for a door, when a hoarse voice shouted, 'What the hell do you think you're doing?'

The voice came from an upper window, where a bald man in shirt sleeves, holding a duster he had apparently been shaking, was looking down at me. His expression was hostile, and I wilted.

'I – I was looking for someone to ask about evening school,' I stuttered.

My questioner looked pained.

'There's not likely to be night school on Saturday afternoon, now is there? You'll have to come on Monday night.' And he started to lower the window.

I did not move. I wanted to ask what time I should come.

He threw the window up again impatiently.

'Now get outta here! We don't want the likes of you hanging around. Get out!'

I got out, and stood in the street quivering with mortification.

Avril, looking like a pocket-sized thundercloud, stamped her foot and said, 'Nasty old man! I don't like him.'

I laughed a little weakly, and looked again at the poster. It said the classes were from 7.30 p.m. to 9.30 p.m.

My mind made up, I went home determined not to be put off by nasty old men.

Father was sitting by the empty fireplace, reading

War and Peace. Without preamble, I mentioned the evening school to him.

He hardly seemed to hear me, and I busied myself making a bit of fire to boil a panful of water for tea.

'Daddy?' I queried again.

At last he said, 'You cannot go to evening school.'

'But, Daddy, why not?' I protested. 'Fiona and you could watch Avril, and I could put Edward to bed before I went. Tony and Brian will go to bed whenever you or Mother tell them.'

His face was wooden, though at the same time sad.

'If you go to evening school, my dear, it will be necessary to state your age and other details. You are not yet fourteen and the school inspectors would order you back to day school.'

'Well, I can't see why I can't go to either day school or evening school,' I said with all the irritating belligerence of a thirteen-year-old. 'Why can't Mother look after Edward and Avril, while I go to school? She's much better now.'

'Mother still isn't fit, you know that. She is doing her very best.' He stopped. The marriage had been far from happy; yet they had stayed together and his anxiety about Mother was based on genuine respect for her. 'Your mother is just able to manage if she goes out into the fresh air or works among adults,' he continued. 'I don't know what might happen to her if she was confined with a whining baby.'

'He doesn't whine,' I exclaimed angrily. 'And I nearly go mad trying to make this beastly fire and buy us enough to eat, and . . . and . . .' I burst into loud crying.

That was the beginning of a tremendous family row, in which everyone joined.

Alan tried to soothe me. 'You could go back to school when Edward's bigger,' he said hopefully.

'Once I am fourteen the school won't take me back,' I screamed in an abandonment of rage.

'Stop making an exhibition of yourself,' said Father. 'When I get a job, you will be able to go to finishing school.'

I looked at him scornfully. French finishing schools were expensive and seemed far removed from the realities of life in Liverpool.

Fiona began to cry. 'Don't be cross with Helen, Daddy.'

'Oh, shut up, Fiona,' I snarled.

'I want my tea,' demanded Avril.

I slapped her.

She immediately began to bellow like a lovesick moose.

This brought Tony hotly to her defence and a smart rebuke to me from Father.

Into the uproar came Mother, weary and hungry.

'What *is* the matter?' she asked, putting down her battered handbag.

'Helen wants to go to evening school and I have told her that it is impractical, because the school inspectors would pick her up as being young enough for day school.'

'Well, why can't I go to day school?'

Mother's lips began to tremble. 'You are needed at home, dear.'

'No, I am not. You can very well look after the children.'

'I have to go to work. The doctor recommended it. And I am the most likely one to get work.'

'I don't believe it,' I said. Thirteen-year-olds can be very cruel.

'The general welfare of the family demands that you stay home.'

'I won't!'

Mother suddenly started to cry hysterically, shrieking that it was too much and I was a hard-hearted, thankless daughter.

'I have nothing to be thankful for,' I retorted bitterly.

'Helen, Helen, don't!' Fiona whispered, her eyes wide and terrified, as she clutched my arm. Alan, from across the room, implored me silently.

The fight went out of me. I turned to Fiona and let her lead me back to our newspaper bed. There, crouched together with my head on her shoulder, I wept myself to exhaustion. I had lost my Waterloo.

By mid-May, Fiona seemed well enough to go back to school. She was by nature placid to the point of apathy, and her gentle pliability made her popular at school. At home, she received no attention and, without playthings, she began to get bored and to ask to be allowed to return to the more lively world of school. My parents had not mentioned school to her. They went out on their various rounds of employment agencies, libraries, etc., and seemed to have forgotten her. I, therefore, prepared her for school one morning as best I could.

At the last moment she balked.

'I feel shy,' she said, standing uneasily in the dark hall and rubbing one foot against the other. 'And I haven't got twopence for the fee. Alan should have waited for me.'

Impatiently I thrust twopence into her hand

from the daily shilling I received to buy food. But still she would not move and stood biting her nails and staring anxiously through the glass door at the busy street.

'Come with me,' she demanded.

In a home as empty as ours, there was little for me to do, so I put Edward and Avril into the Chariot and together we walked the four blocks to school.

The school was a fine, stone building, matching architecturally the adjoining church and presbytery. A high, iron railing surrounded the playground, and we paused by the gate to see if we could find one of Fiona's playmates, so that she would not feel so lonely when going into school.

A pretty lady teacher came hurrying towards the gate. When she saw Fiona she smiled at her through the veil of her smart, little hat.

'Good morning, Fiona. I am glad to see you back. Are you feeling quite well again now? Alan told me that you were in hospital.'

She ran her eyes over Fiona's thin, underclothed body and returned Fiona's angelic, worshipping smile. Then she looked at me in a puzzled fashion. A question trembled on her lips.

Fiona had been brought up properly and she immediately said politely, 'Miss Brough, may I introduce my elder sister, Helen, and this is Avril and this is my baby brother, Edward.'

Miss Brough's brow cleared.

She said, 'How do you do.'

I murmured, 'Very well, thank you.'

'I don't remember you going through our school, my dear,' she remarked to me. 'You must have left before I came – I have only been here three years.' She chucked Edward under the chin with a finger clothed in good brown leather. Then she looked at me again, more sharply. 'But that is not possible – you are quite young.' She laughed. 'You must have gone to school somewhere else.'

My tongue clove to the roof of my mouth and I could not answer.

Fiona said brightly, 'She used to go to our old school. She has never been to school in Liverpool.'

'Haven't you, my dear?'

'No, Miss Brough.'

I was nearly tongue-tied with fear of what my parents would say if they found out about this conversation.

She was looking at me keenly now, and must have seen the stark fright in my eyes. She pursed her delicately painted lips, and said, 'Well, never mind. Fiona, hurry up or you will be late.'

The school bell began to ring and she smiled

reassuringly at me and said, 'Goodbye. Goodbye, Avril and Edward.'

'Goodbye,' I muttered through clenched teeth.

My legs were shaking so much that I could not start the pram. I watched her disappear through the school's ornately carved doorway before, at last, I could make my feet move.

I said nothing to my parents.

A week later a school attendance officer called upon my parents while I was out. How they evaded being prosecuted and sent to prison for my long truancy I will never know. Perhaps their calm authoritative manners made even school attendance officers quail. My immediate attendance was, however, ordered.

I faced two outraged parents every day for the next six weeks until my fourteenth birthday. The day after that, I was back home again looking after Edward.

I had never been to an elementary school, and I found myself far ahead of the other children in the class in everything except mathematics. It was, however, bliss to hold a pencil in my unaccustomed fingers and to try my wits against the work put before me.

This school had a new and enthusiastic drawing-master. He had to teach children who, for the most part, hardly knew that artists created pictures, and he had only pencils, paper and pastel crayons with which to work, but at my first lesson he did his utmost to explain perspective to the disinterested class.

'Any questions?' he asked.

While the rest of the class stared at him glumly, I put up my hand.

'Could you explain why medieval pictures often look so alive and real though they have no perspective?' I asked hopefully.

The class turned round in a body and stared at me open mouthed. The teacher's Adam's apple bobbed up and down as he sought to reply to me.

Finally, he answered me briefly and then set the class the task of drawing a picture of mountains and roads.

He came and sat on the bench beside me and examined my work. He looked carefully at the little picture and suggested a technical method of improving the texture of the shading in it, while I sat in frozen silence beside him afraid that I would smell abominable to him.

'I should like you to draw me one or two more, as homework,' he said at last. 'You can sketch anything which takes your fancy. I want to see what you can do.'

Breathless with excitement, I said I would like to do the drawings but I had neither paper nor pencils.

He smiled and said calmly, 'I can provide you with them.'

I sat on the steps for several evenings, Edward crawling at my feet, while I sketched the life of the street and a picture of Avril, who was hugely flattered at having a drawing made of her.

A week or two later, the drawing-master expressed his approval of my work and produced a small examination paper for me to work my way through. The paper, with my drawings, vanished into officialdom.

'There is a scholarship available at the City School of Art,' he explained kindly to me, 'and I have put you in for it.'

I was happy. For the first time in two years I played with other girls, and I was being taught, though in a rough-and-ready manner. Nobody wanted to sit by me because I was so disgustingly dirty, even by the low standards prevalent in the neighbourhood, but in the open school yard I played tag and skipped until my limited strength gave out.

My fourteenth birthday passed, and my parents put an end to my little holiday. I wept and raged, but to no purpose. I was wanted at home, and Father thankfully turned over Avril and Edward to me again.

Although I had played with other girls at school, I had found nothing in common with them. They had a hearty vulgarity of speech and manner which made me recoil from them and, to them, a girl who spoke as if she had ollies in her mouth was very suspect. A small group of girls who were better behaved and came from better homes regarded me with undisguised horror.

I was back where I had started from, pushing Edward's Chariot to and from the shops or the park, and without any hope of bettering myself.

During the summer holidays, I took all the children to the parks to play, and sat wistfully amongst stout mothers in black shawls, watching my little charges play just as they did. The children accepted me as just another 'Mum' and I was too shy to ask if I could play too.

September saw the children back at school again. I watched them go with envy. Now I was over fourteen I could not hope for further education.

CHAPTER TWENTY-THREE

Alan and I sat huddled together on the front step. The October evening was cold and clammy; yet we were reluctant to go into the stuffy house. The gaslamps' light gleamed softly on the damp pavement and women hurried by, their black shawls held tightly round them, their children whining at their heels. Three young men lolled against the iron railings of the corner house; their noisy laughter mingled with that from the public house on the corner opposite to them. Maurrie, the second-hand clothes man, shuffled by with a sack on his back.

An Irish woman plodded stolidly up the street. Near us, she stepped out into the middle of the street and turned, to take up a belligerent stance facing the front steps of the house opposite.

She was a scarifying-looking person, hugely fat with legs like wool-clad pillars. Her hair was parted across her head from ear to ear and the back part had been plaited and made into a neat bun; the front hair had been parted again down the middle and plaited forwards, the resulting braids being draped down either side of her face and under her ears, to be fastened at the back. The result was outlandishly fierce-looking to anyone unaccustomed to the Victorian hair-styles of some Liverpool Irish women. She smoothed down her white apron over her black skirt, wrapped her black, crocheted shawl around her and folded her enormous arms. Then, gathering her breath until her purple cheeks stood out like balloons, she opened her mouth and screamed.

'Yer pack o' bloody whores!' she yelled at the house Miss Sinford called The House of Sin. 'I'll show yer! Taking a decent woman's hoosband.'

A crowd materialized from nowhere.

'Go it, Ma!' shouted one of the young men from the corner.

There was a flutter of sniggering laughter from the crowd and a murmur of encouragement.

A frail-looking, middle-aged woman, her bare legs thick with varicose veins and her feet shoved into ancient carpet slippers, was unwise enough to open the door and appear on the steps before her.

'You'd better stop that,' she shouted, 'or I'll call a copper.'

This produced such a description of the moral habits of the local constabulary that even the young men in the crowd were impressed. The Irish have a vivid way of expressing themselves, and the shawl woman was no exception. She lifted a fist as stout as a leg of mutton and shook it at the prostitute.

'Yer harlot, yer!' She finished up, and spat accurately at the feet of the Lady of Sin.

Alan giggled behind his hand and whispered, 'Has the lady on the steps taken the other lady's husband from her?'

'Yes,' I said under my breath.

'I'm not surprised. I imagine he ran away from her – she looks as fierce as a tiger.'

I looked at the woman on the steps. She was quite old, her face haggard under its paint. Her hair was dyed a startling red, and diamanté earrings hung from each ear. I was mystified as to where her charm lay. I had read most of Emile Zola's works and now understood the occupation of the ladies opposite. But Zola's heroines were beautiful, and I had always gathered from the conversation of grown-ups that, unless one was beautiful, one did not stand a chance of even a husband, never mind a queue of men such as these ladies commanded.

The woman on the steps drew back towards her front door. She glanced uneasily up and down the street. Several possible clients, hands in pockets, were wandering a trifle unsteadily towards the crowd.

She became anxious to placate, and whined, 'Ah dawn't know who yer hoosband is. Ah dawn't even knaw who yer mean. Na go home,' she wheedled, 'and stop making an exhibition of yerself.'

This infuriated the Irish woman so much that she went up the steps like a tank and punched the small woman in the face.

In a moment, clutched together, they were rolling down the steps and on to the pavement, clawing at each other's eyes, using teeth and knees to inflict as much damage as possible.

The crowd surged forward, roaring approval, and shouting encouragement to whichever participant they favoured.

Three very large dock labourers, who had been standing uneasily watching the exchange, raised their voices against the general hubbub.

'Na, Ma, come on,' they cajoled the Irish woman. 'This is too much. Come on, na. Break it oop!'

But Ma, shawlless and nearly blouseless by now, was too busy holding off the red-haired cat she had provoked to take anybody's advice. Alan and I watched, open-mouthed, through the shifting legs of the crowd.

Suddenly, a little spurt of blood showed on the shawl woman's face, and the crowd hushed.

A male voice said sharply, 'Ee, that's not fair. Get off, you.'

A boot was sharply applied to the prostitute's bottom and she let go immediately, whipped to her feet and whirled on her new assailant.

He backed away from her warily.

'Na, you just take that blade out from under yer thumb-nail, yer lousy bitch.'

The shawl woman heaved herself to her feet, panting. She wiped her face with the back of her hand. When she saw blood on it, she screamed in mixed rage and terror.

'I'll get yer for this!' she shrieked, at the same time putting a little distance between herself and her opponent.

Two of the dockers jumped the prostitute suddenly from behind, caught her arm and twisted it behind her back. While one held her, the other extracted a piece of razor blade from under one of her long nails and held it up for the crowd to see.

There was a threatening murmur.

'Let me go,' she shouted, her voice full of fear.

The men released her and she ran up the steps, her carpet slippers, still on her feet, flapping as they hit the stone.

We became aware of another heated altercation on the edge of the crowd. The pub had closed and its patrons were coming home, among them a huge, bull-necked man who was bellowing, 'Ah'll teach 'er to make a row in t' street, ah will!'

His friends pulled anxiously at his shabby jacket sleeve and murmured, 'Na, then, Bill. Na, then.'

With a sigh of delightful anticipation, the crowd opened to make way for the bull-necked man, while the prostitute vanished into the House of Sin and the sound of a bolt being shot on the inside of the door came clearly across the street.

The bull-necked man charged through the expectant crowd, undoing his trouser belt as he came. His seamed face was red with rage and the muscles and veins of his neck bulged above the neckband of his union shirt. With a smart pull, he whipped his belt out and, swinging it by its buckle, he advanced on the shawl woman, who came towards him, her shawl again draped across her back, but her huge bosom almost bare. She threw back her shoulders to exhibit her ample charm and swayed her hips seductively. Blood still trickled down her cheek but she smiled slyly at the newcomer.

'Na, then, our Mary Ann. What yer think yer doing? I won't stand for it, d' yer hear me!'

She stuck her chin in the air and spat an epithet at him.

Infuriated, he shot out a huge red fist, tore at her bun, took a firm hold on the tumbling plaits and twisted her by her hair till her back was towards him. Then, lifting his belt he brought it down hard on her buttocks. She screamed, and her shawl fell off again, revealing her fat, naked shoulders already scratched in the fight. A second time the belt whistled through the air and a red welt appeared across the buxom shoulders.

I started up with a cry of horror, but one of the women who lived in our house pushed me sharply down on to the step again.

'Let him be,' she hissed. 'She loves it.'

'Loves it?' I hissed back. 'But she's being hurt!' And I winced as the belt cracked down again, and the woman screamed.

The crowd was silent now, tense with the same tenseness of dogs sitting in front of a house where there is a bitch in heat. I felt sick.

The woman from our house said kindly, 'You

go inside and leave the likes of them to themselves.'

Alan and I, both frightened, ran into the hall of our house, from which vantage point we continued to watch.

Beating her steadily, while the shawl woman alternately screamed and cursed, the man was gradually dragging the woman through the crowd and over the cross-road to a smaller house than ours farther down the street, where apparently they lived. He flung her against the closed door and she stood with her back against it, sobbing wildly. The man threw himself against her, and the crowd whooped.

'Go it, Bill,' they shouted.

Bill reached behind his wife and turned the door knob of his home, put his hand on the woman's naked breast and pushed her, so that she seemed to fly backwards into the narrow hall. He followed, and slammed the door after him.

Regretfully, the crowd slowly broke up and departed. Alan and I, both shaking with nervous tension, went slowly up to our apartment.

Fiona was sitting by the window having watched the same scene from a better vantage point. She had evidently been much impressed by the prostitute.

'Wasn't it exciting, Helen? Wasn't the little woman opposite brave to fight that big, fat shawl woman? What were they fighting about?'

'I am not sure,' I said untruthfully.

Fiona said, 'You should draw a picture of it, Helen.'

I laughed.

'I don't think Mummy or Daddy would like me to draw pictures of things like that. Come along, I think you had better go to bed.'

Alan was wandering about the dark room and he came, finally, and stood by us, hands in pockets, looking down at the street which was now practically empty, except for one or two jolly-looking sailors rolling unsteadily up the steps of the House of Sin.

'Why didn't you go to art school, Helen?' Alan asked unexpectedly.

I turned and asked in surprise, 'Art school? What do you mean?'

The response was truly brotherly.

'Art school, stupid. What do you think I meant? You know, when you got the scholarship. I always meant to ask you, but there never seems to be much peace for conversations.'

'Scholarship? I have never won a scholarship, you know that.'

'Heavens, you are dumb! Don't you remember – you sat for it when you got caught and had to go back to school.'

Alan looked at me as if I had lost my reason.

'Oh, that. I didn't get it. I never heard anything about it, after Mr Piper entered my name for it.'

'But – but –' stammered Alan, 'Mr Browning – the headmaster – asked me only the other day how you were getting on, and I meant to ask you what happened. If you got it, why didn't you go to art school? It would have been wonderful for you.'

The episode in the street had left me rather trembly and I sat down suddenly as a horrible suspicion went through my head.

Had I indeed won the scholarship? If I had, my parents would have been informed of it. Had they refused it on my behalf? They were perfectly entitled to do so – schooling was not compulsory after the age of fourteen.

This idea was so repulsive to me that at first I could not accept it. Surely, my parents would realize that it was a wonderful opportunity for me. Surely, they would have my interests at heart. It must be a mistake – I could not have won.

Yet if Alan's headmaster said I had won, won I

had. He would not forget that one of the few scholarships available at that time had been awarded to his school.

'If I won,' I said through clenched teeth, 'I was never told about it.'

'How queer,' said Alan, and Fiona's enormous eyes widened even farther as she, too, considered the matter. 'You'd better ask Mummy or Daddy.'

Such a rush of pain went through my skimpy body that I wrapped my arms around myself and leaned my head nearly down to my knees. In little gasps, I said, 'I don't think I want to ask them. I don't think I can bear to.'

'I'll ask,' said Alan stoutly. 'I'm not afraid.'

'Oh no, Alan,' I said. 'You will only be told that it's none of your business – and the whole family will be upset.'

He knew I was right and was silent.

I was almost certain in my mind that my parents had just not told me because my attendance at school for a prolonged period would have compounded their difficulties; they would have lost their baby-sitter and housekeeper – and they would have had to pay a substitute.

I rocked myself backwards and forwards, as my touching belief that my parents, even if they had not much love for me, would do their best for me, and that they had always done so, died. I was in agony. The research into the ruthless exploitation of the eldest child was still far in the future, and there was no explanation to console my childish despair.

Two bony pairs of arms were quietly wrapped around me, and two young heads came close to mine.

'Never mind, Helen. Please don't cry. What's a silly old scholarship, anyway? You got it. You're clever. You'll get another one some day.'

I did not cry. I could not.

Gently, I told Alan to go to bed.

I pushed Fiona quietly towards our pile of newspapers laid on top of the old door; the papers had an irritating habit of spreading themselves on to the floor as well. I laid myself down on them, facing the wall, and pulled my knees up tight like a baby in the womb. If I took little breaths and lay perfectly still, perhaps the pain inside me would go away.

I slept little, but felt calmer in the morning. The children were dispatched to school. Mother went out. Father hurriedly prepared to go down to the labour exchange. As he struggled to neaten himself, I asked him diffidently, 'Did you ever hear anything about the art scholarship I sat for?'

He looked at me abstractedly. 'Art scholarship?'

'Yes. You remember – the one I sat for while I was at school – just before my birthday.'

He was quiet for a moment and sat staring at his shoelace which had broken.

'Yes,' he said at last. 'We did hear something about it. It couldn't be awarded to you.'

'But did I win?' I asked in a whisper.

'You did. However, when we said that you were born in Cheshire, we were told that you were ineligible and should never have been entered for it. Cheshire comes under a different education committee.'

'Why didn't you tell me about it?'

'There seemed no point – children get upset about these things.'

I nodded. I could not speak because my teeth were chattering so much from the nervous effort I had made to ask about the scholarship.

I hugged Edward to me, while he seized his battered trilby hat and departed. I could hear the loose sole on one of his shoes flipping on each step.

All that morning, I thought about the scholarship. Pressed against the glass-topped biscuit tins in the tiny grocery store, the rancid smell of the bacon-cutting machine enveloping me, I had a long wait in the tiny shop while the grocery woman measured out single ounces of tea, sugar and margarine, climbed her ladder to reach down tins of condensed milk and had long arguments with several desperate women trying to extend their credit with her.

By the time it was my turn to be served with the twopennyworth of rice I wanted, I had come to the conclusion that I must accept my father's explanation, despite the fact that the school had known my place of birth.

CHAPTER TWENTY-FOUR

Dully, sulkily, I continued to look after the children through the winter, trying to dry their rags when they came in rain-soaked, trying to buy with pennies enough food for nine, living in a world where handkerchiefs, toilet-paper, hot water and soap ranked as unobtainable luxuries. Fortunately, the stomach can become accustomed to very little food, and the children did not now cry very often that they were hungry, as long as they had bread and potatoes.

In an effort to make sales and increase their profits, even the more reputable local shopkeepers now cut margarine into quarter pounds, though it cost only fourpence to buy a whole pound, and opened pots of jam to sell at a penny a tablespoonful – bring your own cup. One tiny corner shop, presided over by a skinny harridan whose hands never seemed to have been washed, would make up a pennyworth of almost anything that could be divided up. This resulted in a very high price per pound – but if one has only a penny one has little choice in the matter.

A learned professor published a detailed menu showing that a full-grown man could eat well on four shillings a week but it was of no help to me. Four shillings per week per head to spend on food would have represented to us an unattainable height of luxurious living.

In the city council, a stout, outspoken Labour couple tore into the mayor, aldermen and councillors with bitter tongues on behalf of the unemployed, the homeless and the aged. Mr and Mrs Braddock – our Bessie, as Mrs Braddock was known to many – started a lifelong battle on behalf of the poor of Liverpool. On the docks, the Communists made inroads among the despised and ill-treated dock labourers, the results of which are still apparent in the labour unrest rampant in the docks of Liverpool forty years later.

City health officials looked in despair at horrifying infant mortality rates and at a general death rate nearly the highest in the country. Nobody, of course, died of starvation – only of malnutrition.

The Roman Catholic Church and the Church of England continued to build themselves a cathedral apiece and solicited donations.

My parents at about this time seemed to have given up all hope of any real future and struggled on from one day to the next, too dulled by hunger and privation to plan how they might get out of the morass they were in.

My father tended to sit silently indoors now, only going to the labour exchange and the public assistance committee, because he was more ragged than the most poverty-stricken tramp I ever encountered. My mother still made valiant efforts to keep her appearance reasonable so that she could apply to shops and offices for work.

One sunny Sunday in March, however, Father decided he could stand the rank atmosphere of the house no more and he and Brian went for a walk in the town, which was fairly deserted on Sundays. Father always feared being arrested for vagrancy, but he hoped police would be few and far between on this day of rest.

Two hours later, a petrified Brian came rushing up the stairs and into our living-room, where I was rocking Edward to sleep in his Chariot. He buried his face in my shoulder.

'Daddy's been arrested,' he cried.

I jumped up in alarm and Edward cried out as the rocking ceased.

'Oh, Heavens! Whatever did he do?'

Brian continued to sob in my arms in sheer fright.

'Tell me, Brian. What did he do? Did he steal some cigarettes?'

I felt Brian nod negatively.

'Well, he must have done *something*!'

'He didn't do anything.'

I knelt down and hugged Brian close.

'Well, tell me what happened. Come on, love, tell me.'

Brian's sobs reduced to sniffs and with all the maddening long-windedness of children, he said, 'Well, we walked down into the town and we looked in Cooper's and MacSymon's windows at all the lovely food – they had peaches in brandy in Cooper's. And then we looked in the furniture stores and Daddy showed me a jade idol in Bunney's, at the corner of Whitechapel. Then we walked up Lord Street – opposite Frisby Dykes – and looked at the tailors' shops in North John Street.'

'Yes, yes,' I said impatiently.

'Well, then Daddy wanted to look at the gentlemen's shops in the arcade in Cook Street – and it was at the corner of Cook Street that we saw this strange man.'

'What kind of a strange man?'

'Well, he was big and nicely dressed with lovely polished boots. Daddy said he was a plain-clothes policeman – and we were both a bit scared – but Daddy said to keep on walking as if there was nothing wrong.' Brian wiped his nose on the cuff of his jersey. 'So we did – and we looked at all the pipes and tobacco and suits and things and this man started to walk up behind us.'

'What did you do?'

'We started to walk faster and faster and when we got to Castle Street and turned the corner, we ran like anything and the man ran after us. Daddy pushed me into a doorway by a pillar and told me to stay there, and he went on running. When the policeman had passed me by, I peeped out – and the policeman had his hand on Daddy's shoulder like they do in books.' Brian burst into tears again. 'So I doubled back down Cook Street and came home.' he wailed.

'Never mind, Brian. I am sure Daddy will be all right. It is probably a mistake. We'll tell Mummy about it. You just wait here a minute.'

Mother was taking a little nap in the bedroom and I was very afraid that if I woke her with Brian's story she would have one of her periodic outbursts of temper, or perhaps have hysterics; but she sat on the edge of the old mattress while she considered it, and then said quite sensibly, 'I don't think we can do anything except wait. We don't know which police station he is in. I expect they will let us know what he is charged with.'

Her calmness calmed Brian and me, and he went off to play with Tony, while I went back to my book. I could not read, however. I realized suddenly how much officialdom Father coped with on our behalf. Without him, we were defenceless against those who would put us in the workhouse.

I began to shake with fear, fear for my father and terror at the inhumanity of the workhouse.

CHAPTER TWENTY-FIVE

Edward had been put to bed, and Mother and I sat on our two chairs staring out of the window, united by our worry over Father. Occasionally, there was a steady clang-clang and flashes of electricity from behind the houses opposite as tram cars a couple of streets away swayed around a corner. The irate 'whip-whip-whip' of a naval vessel making its way upriver competed with the noise of the trams, and, in the far distance, the shunting yard at Edge Hill lent a background of clanking to the other sounds. No cars passed – the district was too poor for anything more ambitious than a horsedrawn milk cart. A boy came by on a bicycle and two giggling girls paused to gossip under the gaslight outside.

A car drew up outside our house so quietly that

we were at first unaware of its presence. Someone got out.

'Good night, and – thank you very much.'

It was Father. His voice was unmistakable.

We jumped up as the front door slammed in the distance. We could hear Father's laborious step on the stairs. He was whistling 'It's a long way to Tipperary'.

Never had the old tune sounded so welcome. If he could whistle, things were not that bad. We ran to the top of the stairs, six small grey ghosts and one adult, and peered over the banisters.

'Hello, children. Is Brian safely home?'

'Yes,' we chorused. 'What happened to you?'

Father emerged from the darkness of the stairwell. He was smiling broadly and his step was jaunty.

'It's a long story. Come in and I'll tell you.'

He even smiled at his wife, I noticed, and I could see in the small light from the street the sudden, unreasoned hope spring in Mother's eyes when she saw Father's cheerful expression.

'Come in. I have lots to tell you, and you are all old enough to hear it.'

He led us, like the Pied Piper, into the living-room.

'Tell us,' we implored, hunger, filth, misery forgotten.

Father made the most of his moment. He settled himself in a chair and took Avril on his knee. He was still beaming.

He cleared his throat.

'I expect Brian told you about our walk.'

'Yes,' we said impatiently.

'What happened when the policeman caught you?' asked Brian.

'He wanted to see my tie.'

'Your tie?' exclaimed Mother.

'Yes, my old All Saints tie. I thought he was mad, but I was afraid to do anything else but pull it out and show it to him.'

Avril shoved herself around on Father's lap and pulled out the sad remains of his old school tie. It looked the same as usual.

'When he saw it, he opened his own overcoat at the neck, and he was wearing the same tie – I mean a nice, new version of it.'

Alan whistled.

'He asked me how I came to be down and out.

'"It is a long story," I told him. Suddenly, my legs began to give under me – we had walked a very long way, you know, and I get faint very easily these days. He saw that I was feeling ill, and said it didn't matter.

'"Come and sit in the car for a few minutes," he said. "I have to wait for a colleague who has business in this building here."

'I was thankful to get into the car and sit down. Almost immediately his colleague came and was surprised to find me in the car – I suppose he thought the man on the beat would normally deal with vagrants like me. However, my friend of the tie put the car into gear and said that we were going to go to the police canteen.

'"Don't get the wind up," he said to me. "I think you can do with a meal."

'I felt too weak to care what happened to me, but a meal sounded a wonderful idea. So away we went to the police station and through to the canteen.' He paused reminiscently, and then went on, 'He stood me a full meal – stew and steamed pudding.'

'Delicious,' we murmured enviously.

'And when I had finished, he gave me a cigarette, and he seemed such a decent sort that I told him about everything that happened to us.

'He did not interrupt me once – and his friend sat and watched me. At the end they looked at each other – and mulled over what I had said.

'He asked me quite a lot about our school, and then said he remembered me. He left All Saints the year after I was sent there, but he recollected that blow on the head I got from a cricket ball; it caused a good deal of consternation because I took a long time to come round and they were not able to get a doctor for some time.'

'Childhood episodes do stick in one's mind,' said Mother.

I looked at her in surprise. It had never occurred to me that she understood the world of children or that she had been a child herself. Nanny was the person who understood children.

Father continued, 'He said he thought he could get me a job with the City.'

'Really?' queried Mother, frank disbelief in her voice.

'Yes. I told him that I had made every endeavour to obtain employment – but now I was so shabby it was impossible. I said frankly that the rags he saw me in were all I had, that I had not even soap to wash myself with.

'And do you know what he said then? It was most unexpected.'

'No?' we breathed.

'He said the school would undoubtedly outfit me from their benevolent fund – I used to subscribe to that, you know, but I never thought of it in connection with myself. He is going to write tonight to ask for immediate help. Meantime, he is going to talk to the City about me.'

'How wonderful,' Alan cried.

'Yes, it is,' said Mother.

Fiona began to cry slowly; they were tears of relief. Her illness had left her with practically no stamina, but she rarely complained and, I believe, most of the family hardly realized she existed.

She was a great contrast to her lively, noisy younger sister, who now said unsympathetically, 'Oh, shut up, Fiona. You're supposed to be glad, not sad!' And cuddling up to Father, she inquired, 'Shall we be able to have a roast joint?'

We all laughed, and afterwards, we sat up late while we discussed every detail of this miraculous encounter. Even Mother was quite excited and animated about it.

The days dragged by, however, and nothing happened. Father stood in his queues; Mother got two days' work, looking after a special photography display in a store which found that cameras were a slow-moving item amid the general penury in the city. We ate fish and chips one night as a result of this windfall, and Mother was able to buy some stockings, makeup, etc., so that she could look more respectable and, therefore, more employable. We always despaired about our lack of simple articles, like scissors, combs, hair grips, things one takes for granted in a normal home.

At last, when we had given up standing on the front steps waiting for the postman and the spring had again gone out of Father's step, the plain-clothes man called in person. He was let in by Miss Sinford, who fortunately did not connect him with the police, and he clumped up to our evil-smelling den.

Father was out.

Mother received him with her usual grace and sat down on one chair, while he, in response to her invitation, lowered himself cautiously on to the other. Most of the children were at school; Avril, Edward and I, however, stood in a group and stared goggle-eyed at our saviour.

All Saints School, the visitor said with a friendly grin, had made a grant sufficient to outfit Father completely, provided he shopped carefully. He stopped, his beefy face showing some concern. 'Er – the school has asked me to administer the grant – and – er – I hate to say this – they want me to go with your husband to shop. Now, I don't mind in the least – but I hope he won't be offended.'

'I am sure he won't,' said Mother with unusual briskness. 'However, you will appreciate that he is in no state to go out with you – or enter a decent shop.' Her voice broke, and she looked as if she was going to weep. She recovered herself, however, and said as she studied her chapped, unmanicured hands, 'Do you think the grant committee would mind giving enough money first to buy some soap for a bath – and a haircut?'

The plain-clothes man leaned forward and patted her hand.

'I am sure that would be all right. I do understand – you know, in my job I see a lot of things.' He thought for a moment, and then added, 'The public swimming-baths have also places where you can take a full bath – I think it costs sixpence – and they provide soap and towels, as well.'

I marvelled that a man whose life had obviously been comfortable, should understand that it was likely we had no towels.

'Oh, how lovely,' I said impetuously, only to be silenced by an icy look from Mother.

I could hear Father dragging himself slowly up our endless staircase, and, picking up Edward, I ran to meet him and whispered about the visitor.

When Father entered, the man rose courteously and held out his hand. Father clasped it. I doubt if anyone had felt that his hand was worth shaking since our arrival in Liverpool.

Father's fatigue fell away from him. It was arranged that the policeman would buy some underwear and bring it to us. He also said gently that, if Father would accept them, he could bring a pair of flannels and an old tweed jacket from his own home, so that Father could go into a store without embarrassment to choose a suit and raincoat.

It was obvious that Father felt his humiliation very deeply. His face was sadder than I had ever seen it. He appreciated, however, the great kindness of this police officer on whom he had no other call than that they had attended the same public school, and he thanked him gratefully for his thoughtfulness.

'I have tentatively arranged for you to see this man in the Municipal Buildings at ten o'clock next Friday morning,' said our friend, standing up and handing Father a slip of paper.

Father nodded, took the slip of paper and carefully laid it on the dusty mantelpiece.

'I don't know how I am going to repay you for all this,' he said.

'Don't mention it,' said the plain-clothes man cheerfully. 'Very glad to be able to help – put it down to the old school tie!'

The underwear, trousers, jacket and a shirt arrived in a brown paper parcel, addressed to Father and left on our landing. When I asked our incorrigible old lookout, Miss Sinford, who had delivered the parcel, she insisted that nobody had called at the house that day. I can only imagine that someone like the milkman, who still brought Edward his pint of milk, must have been asked to bring them in, so as to avoid a police car being yet again stationed outside the house. Miss Sinford would not have counted the milkman as being a person; like the postman, the public assistance visitor and the poor, he was always with us.

Armed with five shillings given him for the purpose, Father went to the public baths and found that, indeed, a spotlessly clean bath, towels and soap, not to speak of hot water, were all his for the sum of sixpence. Apparently, he spent so much time in the bath that the attendant threatened to charge him another sixpence or empty the bath if Father did not come out.

He dressed himself in his clean clothes, rolled up his rags into a bundle, except for his broken-down shoes, which he had, perforce, to retain, dumped the bundle into a litter-bin outside the baths, and went for a shave and a haircut.

When he came home, I hardly knew him.

Although the jacket and pants were too large for him and his shoes were a mess, he had an aura of respectability about him that did more for our spirits than anything heretofore.

There was still some money left from the five shillings, and Father sent Alan and Fiona to buy fish and chips and peas and a packet of cigarettes. I hoped that All Saints School did not learn, by some extraordinary means, that we had spent two and sixpence of their money on food instead of on outfitting Father, and, even worse, sixpence on cigarettes.

The detective picked Father up two days later, and they went together to buy a good ready-made suit, another shirt, a raincoat and a pair of shoes.

It seemed to Alan and me that we had got our Father back from the dead, because he now looked to us as he had done before we came to Liverpool, except that he had shrunk considerably.

Without any difficulty, Father got the clerical post for which he was interviewed – the detective was apparently sufficient reference. He was infinitely better educated and more widely experienced in the business world than the type of clerk the City was normally able to command, and, except when it came to running his own affairs, had a clear and analytical mind.

Though the post was a temporary one, he soon discovered that many of his colleagues had been 'temporary' for ten years or more – it saved the impoverished City from having to provide pensions for them.

He served the city of his birth faithfully and well. Later, he became part of its permanent staff, and, when his department was taken over by the Government as part of the new National Health scheme, he became a civil servant and gradually worked his way upwards. He was never very well-to-do again; on the other hand, he was never again reduced to penury, and he managed to enjoy the latter part of his life in a modest way.

CHAPTER TWENTY-SIX

It seemed reasonable to assume that Father's going to work would make a considerable difference to our standard of living and, consequently, to my own life. The hope that had sustained me through all our bad times had been pinned on this one point. Now, at last, perhaps I would be allowed to go to evening school or take some kind of work and Mother would take her rightful place at home. Life, however, went on exactly as before as far as Edward and I were concerned.

There was no more money to spend on food than there had been before. Wages were so low in Liverpool that Father did not earn much more than he had received when unemployed; the difference was swallowed up in tram fares, lunches and cigarettes – and, of course, the need to keep himself clean and tidy.

Childish hopes waxed again when Mother began to get more regular employment; she was proving to be an excellent saleswoman and was recommended by one employer to another for moving specially difficult merchandise. If she must work, I argued, she might soon earn enough to employ a girl to look after Edward and so release me. In her case also, however, she had first to meet her expenses and then extend her wardrobe so that she looked decent enough to continue work.

Father's being employed sparked a desire in my parents to find a better place in which to live. It had been hopeless even to consider this while he was unemployed – no landlord was prepared to rent a house to an unemployed man with seven children. A city clerk was a different matter, and they finally obtained a neat-looking terrace house with three bedrooms, a sitting-room and a living-room. It had no bathroom, and the water-closet was at the far end of a soot-begrimed back yard. Cooking was done on an old-fashioned coal range in the living-room. It was unfurnished and the rent was seventeen shillings a week. It was a great improvement upon our present accommodation, though not to be compared with the home we had abandoned to our creditors. The relief from climbing stairs was tremendous and, of course, we would save ten shillings a week in rent.

Moving was not difficult as we had almost nothing to move, and suddenly it seemed as if we needed everything much more than we had done before – I suppose it was because we had a whole house to ourselves.

There are always sharks willing to oblige the foolish. In their eagerness to become once more established, my parents bought a set of drawing-room furniture and curtains for the whole house on hire purchase. A hint that we needed beds met with a sharp rebuke. An iniquitous system of 'cheques' enabled them to purchase bedding, crockery and kitchen tools, all of which we badly needed. The cheques, however, were peddled by finance companies and consisted of a permit to buy a given amount of goods from a limited list of stores at greatly inflated prices. Repayment and interest were collected in weekly instalments by the companies' agents. The goods rarely lasted until they were paid for and the rate of interest was high. This type of indebtedness was very prevalent in Liverpool.

This plunge into debt meant that Mother had to work, whether she wished to or not, and I had to care for the children. My little faint hope which had lighted my way through so much was doused, and dark clouds of melancholy gathered round me and were made worse by indifferent health. I watched as the heavy weekly payments drained away money urgently needed for clothing and food. Sufficient did trickle down to buy new running-shoes for the older children; but Edward and Avril had the Chariot to ride in and I did not have to go anywhere except to the shops.

Avril started school in September and Alan would be leaving it at Christmas, a poignant reminder that everybody was making a little progress except me. Would Edward and I always be chained together? Would our needs always be at the bottom of the family's list? Would I always be hungry?

My despair was abysmal. I felt I had no one to turn to for comfort or help. Even hours of weeping as I went about my household tasks failed to relieve the depression which engulfed me.

My father had spent some time talking with Alan about what he would do when he finished school, and it had been agreed that he would try for a job as office boy in a firm where there was a certain amount of training given and where he might sit professionally set examinations. Amongst other openings, this gave him a choice of estate agencies, banking and shipping firms. A bright fourteen-year-old could do better than his forty-year-old father, as far as choice of jobs was concerned.

Nobody asked me what I would like to do. My role in life had been silently decided for me. It was obvious that my parents had no intention of allowing me to be anything but an unpaid, unrespected housekeeper. With all the passion of a fifteen-year-old, I decided that such a life was not worth living.

A foggy September day saw Edward being pushed in the Chariot along the gently heaving Georges Landing-Stage. The Birkenhead ferry was slowly leaving the stage and vanishing into the misty river. The shore hands were coiling up their ropes ready for the next ferry-boat. Upon the invisible river invisible ferries clanged their bells and were answered by freighters sounding their foghorns. Behind me, the lights of the Royal Liver and Cunard buildings barely penetrated the unseasonable gloom. At one end of the landing-stage a pilot-boat had just returned from beyond the bar, after collecting the pilot from an out-going ship. At the other end a group of customs officers chatted, their raincoats gleaming with moisture. No passengers were waiting for the ferries.

Carefully, I tucked the cover round the sleeping Edward and made sure that the hood protected him from the slight wind which occasionally lifted the fog. I hoped someone kind would find him and take him home and love him. I propped the pram against a post so that it could not roll into the water, and left it.

Very slowly, I approached the chain fence that stopped pedestrians from falling off the edge of the landing-stage. When I felt its cold links against my shins, I paused. Some three feet still separated me from the swirling water, invisible for the moment because of the mist.

I stepped over the fence and took a couple of paces more. I could see the water now. Everyone in Liverpool knew that if anybody fell into the water at the end of the landing-stage the tremendous undertow would suck them right under the stage to certain death. It would not take long.

I was shivering violently, nauseated by the thought of the oily water and the choking death which seemed to be the only available way of committing suicide. At the same time I could not bear the thought of turning back into a life which was unendurable to me.

I took a large breath preparatory to jumping.

A huge paw clamped suddenly down on my

shoulders and a voice behind me said, 'And phwhat in the Name o' God do you think you're doing?'

The sudden interruption was so terrifying that my knees buckled under me, and another huge hand grasped the back of my dress, and I was yanked bodily back over the fence.

Supported only by the iron grip on my shoulder, I found myself looking at the middle fastenings of a sailor's waterproofs. I followed the line of the fastenings upwards with my eyes and found myself looking into the rubicund face of the pilot who had just landed. The water dripping off the peak of his cap did not obscure the concern in his eyes.

I could not answer. I was fainting.

'Mother of Heaven, you gave me a fright,' he said sharply.

I must have fainted completely, because the next thing I remember was being in a little canteen and having hot tea forced between my lips by a careworn woman in grubby white.

'Och, you'll be all right now,' she said in a rich Irish voice. 'Sure, and you frightened the Captain out of his wits.'

I put my head down on the tea-stained table by me until the world ceased whirling round me. I felt dreadfully cold and so tired that all I could think about was sleep.

After a minute or two, I straightened up. My rescuer said heartily, 'Well, now, you'll be all right. And don't you step over that chain again, young lady, or you'll fall right in.' He turned to the hovering waitress, put his hand in his trouser pocket, took out a coin and gave it to her. 'Here's for the tea. I've no doubt the gel will be all right in a minute or two. I have to report to the office.'

He looked down at me, his face beaming.

'Goodbye, young lady.'

'Goodbye,' I said, 'and thank you.'

I drank the rest of the tea gratefully and, at the urging of the waitress, sat for about ten minutes to rest. Gradually, my numbed brain began to work once more. I knew I could not screw up enough courage to go out into the fog and try to jump again; yet I could not stay long where I was.

I suddenly remembered Edward.

It seemed that I would have to go home, because there was nowhere else to go.

Slowly I got up, thanked the waitress and, with many protestations that I was now quite well, I went to collect the Chariot. Edward was sitting up and whimpering.

The children were home when I arrived, slowly dragging the Chariot after me.

'You haven't got tea ready,' said Avril indignantly, 'and Alan can't find a knife to cut the bread.'

CHAPTER TWENTY-SEVEN

Very few people who try to commit suicide really want to kill themselves; their attempt is a last hysterical cry for help. When willing hands are outstretched to aid them and some effort is made to alter the circumstances that drove them to such despair, they will try again to cope with life. I was no exception; two people had been very kind to me and I was extremely touched by the fact. On my return home, the necessity of dealing with the children's needs steadied me and Fiona's loving help with these tasks comforted me. I clung to her when we went to bed and drew some strength from the touch of her frail body and from her gentle spirit. By morning, something of my normal common sense had returned.

The day was as bright and clear as its predecessor

had been foggy and damp. The family dispersed to school and to work, Avril going proudly to school holding Fiona's hand. Edward and I were left to contemplate a bare house, except for our shiny new drawing-room, which I dusted very carefully from time to time. The few dishes were soon washed, what beds and substitutes for beds we had were soon tidied and the fire allowed to go out until evening. Though still very exhausted, my spirits rose a little as Edward and I went out to buy food.

Outside the elementary school a fresh poster announced the opening of evening schools that day for the winter session. I contemplated it with a feeling of hopelessness. It would certainly be inconvenient to my parents if I was out in the evening – they would almost certainly veto any such idea.

The hopelessness gave way to a slow burning anger, and then to determination. I would try once more to go to school. Perhaps if Father and Mother were faced with a *fait accompli*, they would give in. I therefore took Fiona and Alan into my confidence at tea-time, and they agreed to help with Edward and Avril while I was away and to cover up for me if my parents noticed my absence.

When both parents went out to the library, I

slipped away to the school and joined a crowd of youngsters moving slowly through the entrance.

A young teacher asked me, as I stood uncertainly in the hall, what courses I wanted to take.

I was aghast. I had no idea what courses to take. All I wanted was to continue my education from where I had left off nearly three years earlier.

'I am not sure,' I managed to mutter. 'I know I need to learn arithmetic.'

She pointed to an open doorway farther down the hall.

'Try bookkeeping,' she said kindly, as she turned to attend to another lost youngster.

I did not know what bookkeeping was, but I was so scared of the shifting, staring young people crowding round me, some of whom sniggered when they looked at me, that I bolted down the corridor and turned thankfully into a classroom holding about a dozen boys and girls and a young lady teacher.

The classroom, with its walls of frosted glass and varnished wood, had enough desks, made to accommodate two pupils each, to swallow about fifty children; four electric lights hanging from the ceiling failed to illuminate it adequately; the bare wooden floor was grey from years of tramping boots. Facing the pupils' desks was a high, single desk for the teacher and near it stood a blackboard on an easel. The air smelled of chalk dust and damp woollens. A dingy, uninspiring room it was, but it was made more lively by the buzz of conversation among the pupils.

As I came through the door, the teacher looked up, and a pall of silence fell upon the gathering. The mouths of the neatly clad, well-scrubbed young people fell open. Then a well-curled blonde began to giggle. She hastily stuffed her handkerchief into her mouth, while a derisive grin spread through the class.

The dim electric lights became blurred, as tears of realization welled up. I must have been a horrible sight, with hair draggling round my shoulders, its greasiness combed through with my fingers; septic acne sores all over my face; hands with dirty, broken nails, sticking out from an ancient cardigan with huge holes in its elbows, no blouse, and a gym slip shiny with accumulated grime. Red blotches of bug bites were clearly visible on my naked legs and thighs, our new house being equally as verminous as our old one, and my toes stuck out of the holes in the laceless gym shoes on my feet.

I fought back my tears. I was made of better stuff than the children before me. My family had been fighting England's battles while theirs were still serfs fit only to keep pigs. I would show them.

Lifting my ugly hooked nose into the air I stared calmly back at them. Gradually, the grins were replaced by uneasy looks and they began self-consciously to talk to each other again.

There ought to be a special medal for understanding teachers. I do not know what prompted the small, perfumed occupant of the teacher's podium to come down from her perch, put her arm around my shoulders, regardless of the fact that I was obviously verminous, and say sweetly, 'Do you want to take bookkeeping, too, my dear?'

She was taken aback visibly when I answered her in my clearest English – she must have expected a strong Liverpool accent.

'I had hoped to learn arithmetic, ma'am. Do you teach it?'

She recovered herself and guided me to an unoccupied double desk at the front of the class, as she replied.

'No. This school has only commercial courses – it is assumed that you will have done the necessary arithmetic already in day-school.'

The other children were again staring at me, and she turned to them and said sharply, 'Please fill in the forms I have given to you. I will take them in in a few minutes.' She turned back to me. 'Now,' she said, 'what kind of arithmetic do you want to learn?'

I explained my lack of algebra, that my academic training had come to an end at a chapter called 'Compound Interest', and that was as much as I knew.

She sat casually on the desk in front of me and looked me over thoughtfully.

'When did you leave school?' she asked.

I explained about leaving school when I was twelve and the subsequent glorious six weeks I had enjoyed just before my fourteenth birthday, and about Edward and Avril and the family.

'I see,' she said, drawing her pale blue cardigan more tightly around her. 'Do you want to train for any particular occupation?'

An occupation seemed so far away, so unattainable, that I said hastily, 'I have not thought of anything special – except that I would like to be able to help the hungry, unemployed people round me.'

She smiled at this and suggested, after some consideration, that I should take the standard commercial course, in which she taught bookkeeping. In addition, she would guide me through a basic course in arithmetic and algebra, which I could do as part of my homework.

'If you take the commercial course, it will form a basis for several different ways of earning a living,' she said practically.

I agreed because it seemed that I had no choice and, at least, she had opened a tiny door of hope for me. Yesterday there had been no hope; today there was a faint gleam.

She lent me her pen and I filled in the form she gave me, while the other members of the class handed theirs in, had them checked and were told to report back two nights later to commence their instruction.

When the classroom had emptied, I went to the teacher's desk and handed in my form.

'Fine,' she said cheerfully. 'Now, that will be half a crown; and here is a list of books you will need. They will cost about ten and sixpence.'

I was stunned. My tiny hope door slammed shut. I managed to gasp out, 'I did not know there was a fee for evening school – I thought it was like elementary day-school – provided by the city – so – so I haven't brought any money.'

The amounts were so small; but they might just as well have been hundreds of pounds, because I did not have them.

The teacher was collecting her papers, and she replied, without looking up, 'Well, never mind. Ask your mother to give you the fee for next time – and you can get the books from any bookshop sometime during the week. Now, be here on Thursday at 7.30, remember.'

'Yes, ma'am,' I said heavily. 'Good night – and thank you.'

I turned and marched out.

As soon as I was outside the school, I rushed to a corner behind a buttress of the building where the street lamps' rays did not penetrate, and, putting my face against the damp, red bricks of the wall, I cried hopelessly and helplessly until not another tear would come. I cried from the frightful pent-up tension of yesterday and the disappointment and humiliation of today. I cried because I was drifting helplessly on a sea of life for which I had not been prepared and which I did not understand. I cried for the perfect peace and safe refuge of my grandmother's house by the sea. I cried because I could not cross the Mersey to reach the green fields and wild seashores I loved.

Frozen and exhausted, I stuffed my blue hands into my cardigan pockets and turned towards home.

I took two steps and stopped. In my pocket was a hard little card. Mother's library card!

Books! Perhaps the library had the books I

needed. If they had, I could keep on reborrowing them, I argued. If it was not yet nine o'clock, I could run to the library and look.

I tore through the streets, taking shortcuts through every alleyway I could, regardless of danger. Dogs barked and cats and rats scampered away at the sound of my thudding feet.

I squeezed into the library's muggy warmth five minutes before closing-time, the list of books clutched in one hand.

Feverishly, I sought through the index. Had they got them? Had they?

They had.

A few minutes later, I emerged, equipped with text-books.

At home I poured out my adventures to Alan and Fiona. It was a long time since I had had such a conversation with any of the family, and they were jubilant about the enrolment and the books. Alan offered to lend me his pen each evening.

'If you don't remind them, perhaps they'll forget that you owe them half a crown,' he said hopefully, in reference to the school fee.

'They will have to,' I said woodenly, 'because I am going to school, no matter what happens.'

Brave words, but I still needed at least one notebook, and, as I put the family to bed, I worried more about obtaining twopence to buy a notebook than I worried about the half-crown.

On Wednesday, I found a piece of comb in a gutter and painfully attacked my tangled mop of hair with it. Mother had a tiny pocket-comb, which of a necessity she had kept for herself, because she could not make herself neat for work if the precious object was broken. Father was fortunately almost bald. The children went uncombed and, mostly, unwashed, until more regular work enabled Mother to buy a strong comb for use by the family.

If ever I became rich, I told myself savagely, I would help to provide a basic kit for the more unfortunate of this world. It would consist of a large bar of kitchen soap, a pile of old white cloth, a pile of newspapers (newspapers can be made into beds, handkerchiefs, toilet-paper, warm padding under thin garments, draught excluders, makeshift window-pane replacements, firing, and a thousand other uses), some razor blades, for beards and nails, and a comb. One has to be without such small amenities to appreciate their worth.

My appearance was not much improved when I again presented myself at school, quailing at the thought of not being able to pay the fee.

The bookkeeping teacher was as kind as before

and, after she had given the class some work to do, she brought over to me a small arithmetic textbook, told me to take it home, read the instructions in the first chapter and see if I could work my way through the problems based on them. She promised to mark the work for me.

Several children had no notebooks, so she provided some paper both for their work and mine. I soon became absorbed in the struggle to make my sluggish brain work, and forgot the silent distaste with which my fellow students were treating me.

Halfway through the evening, the class was taken over by a thin, energetic teacher who was to instruct us in English grammar. She proved equally as friendly and as helpful as the bookkeeping teacher.

Evening school has a long tradition in Lancashire and all over the city classrooms were crowded with young people desirous of improving their education. Again I was following in the footsteps of the humble weavers about whom my old gentleman in the park had told me.

It was Fiona who, accidentally, let fall one evening the information to my parents that I had gone to evening school.

They were rightly angry that I had taken such

action without consulting them and both stormed at me about it.

It would have brought more wrath down upon my head if I had defended myself by saying that I had long since concluded that consultation was waste of time, so I just stated firmly, 'I have been going to evening school and I'm going to continue going.' I had nothing to lose but my chains.

'Where did you get the money from?' asked Mother suddenly, her voice full of suspicion.

I had to own up that I owed the Liverpool education committee two shillings and sixpence – and, worse still, I needed two shillings more for bookkeeping books and other notebooks.

This led to further recrimination, and, with unusual impudence, I asked, 'Would you prefer that I stole it rather than owed it?'

Such insolence was so unlike me, that it brought my parents up short.

Mother said quietly, in a tone more normal than anything she had used since we had arrived in Liverpool, 'No, we would not. Probably we shall manage to find the money somehow.'

This sudden reasonableness frightened me more than if she had had hysterics. I had become so used to her being ill and being unable to pay normal attention to us, that I had forgotten that new hope had recently entered her life and was helping her to get better quite rapidly. Once I had got over the shock and stopped staring at her, round-eyed and fearful, I was piteously grateful.

The following Tuesday evening, hair neatly combed into a bun held with a piece of string, and wearing Fiona's cardigan, which was reasonably clean, I ran through the dank September evening to school. Hot in the palm of my hand was a half-crown, the most important coin I was ever to possess. I was to spend seven years in evening schools and I managed in each subsequent year to win a small scholarship, which covered the increasing fees and my books, as I advanced through the system; so that I did not cost my parents anything more.

The electric lights had already been turned on in the school and a great shaft of light blazed out across the pavement from the main doorway. It was early and no one else was entering. I looked up the stone steps, hollowed out by hundreds of feet, through the hall and up the staircase to the second floor.

The welcoming doorway was my hoping door; the worn stone steps my ladder to the stars. Kind hands, earnest people, were there to help me up them.

I bared my yellow teeth in a smile of pure happiness, charged across the threshold and galloped up the stairs.

Liverpool Miss

Helen Forrester

The continuing story of Helen Forrester's poverty-stricken childhood in Liverpool during the Depression. The Forrester family are slowly winning their fight for survival. But fourteen-year-old Helen's personal battle is to persuade her parents to allow her to earn her own living, to lead her own life after the years of neglect and inadequate schooling while she cared for her six younger brothers and sisters. Her untiring struggles against illness, caused by severe malnutrition, dirt (she has her first bath in four years), and above all the selfish demands of her parents make this true story of courage and perseverance heart-breaking yet heart-warming.

'Records of hardship during the Thirties or earlier are not rare, but this has features that make it stand apart.' *Observer*

'An impressive record of what it is like to be very poor . . . written with a simplicity which is moving and memorable.'
Homes and Gardens

'The story of a young girl's courage and perseverance against adversity . . . warm-hearted and excellent.'
Manchester Evening News

ISBN 0 00 636494 2

By the Waters of Liverpool

Helen Forrester

The third volume in the classic story of Helen Forrester's childhood and adolescence in Liverpool during the 1930s.

Helen has managed to achieve a small measure of independence. At seventeen, she has fought and won two bitter battles with her parents, the first for the right to educate herself at evening classes, the second for the right to go out to work. Her parents are still as financially irresponsible as ever, wasting money while their children lack blankets, let alone proper beds, but for Helen the future is brightening as she begins to make friends of her own age and to develop some social life outside the home. At twenty still never kissed by a lover, Helen meets a strong, tall seaman and falls in love.

'A fascinating autobiography which has also gained a new topicality . . . highly gripping and entertaining'

Birmingham Post

'The most remarkable feature is the author's total lack of bitterness and the quiet humour which she can bring to the most harrowing events' *Times Educational Supplement*

'Should be long and widely read as an extraordinary human story and social document' *Observer*

ISBN 0 00 636540 X

Lime Street at Two

Helen Forrester

'An extraordinary autobiographical document' *Observer*

Helen Forrester continues the moving story of her early poverty-stricken life with an account of the war years in blitz-torn Liverpool, and the happiness which she so nearly captured but which was to elude her twice.

In 1940 Helen, now twenty, reeling from the news that her fiancé Harry has been killed on an Atlantic convoy, is working long hours at a welfare centre in Bootle, five miles from home. Her wages are pitifully low, and her mother claims the whole of them for the housekeeping. Then early in 1941 she gets a new job, and begins to enjoy herself a little. But in May the bombing starts again and another move brings more trouble to Helen, trouble which will be faced, as ever, with courage and determination.

'Remarkable that from so bleak and unloving a background came a writer of such affectionate understanding and unsettling honesty' *Sunday Telegraph*

'What makes this writer's self-told tale so memorable? . . . An absolute recall, a genius for the unforgettable detail, the rare chance of subject' *The Good Book Guide*

ISBN 0 00 637000 4

Madame Barbara

Helen Forrester

An intensely moving tale of loss and love set in post-Second World War England and France.

It is spring 1948 and Barbara Bishop, a young widow from Merseyside, has arrived in Normandy to visit the grave of the husband she hardly knew. Driving her to the cemetery in a battered taxi is Michel Benion, a former poultry farmer, who lost his home and his livelihood in the invasion and is now struggling to support his elderly mother and dying brother.

As they spend time together, attraction grows between Barbara and Michel and quickly turns to passion. Suddenly they seem to have the prospect of a new life opening up before them. But there are many difficulties to be overcome if they are to find happiness together.

A touching love story, a compelling portrayal of the aftermath of war and above all a testament to the courage and endurance of ordinary people, *Madame Barbara* will delight Helen Forrester's countless fans.

ISBN 0 00 651348 4

A Cuppa Tea and an Aspirin

Helen Forrester

A poignant novel of fortitude in the face of unimaginable deprivation, and a celebration of the spirit of a community and a vanished way of life.

Court No. 5, near the Liverpool docks, is one of the worst slums in Europe but, for the dozen families who live there, the warmth of friends and neighbours is a constant, as they share in the hardships and small triumphs of their relentless fight for survival. For women like Martha Connolly, each day is a struggle, and Martha must use all her ingenuity to feed and clothe her nine children in the face of the constant threat of hunger and disease.

In 1938, rumours of a war reach the court and soon it's clear that the coming hostilities will change things for ever. Hard though it is, this is the only life that Martha has ever known – can she prevent it being swept away?

'A writer of such affectionate understanding and unsettling honesty.' *Sunday Telegraph*

0 00 715694 4